Rosenberg Associates Edition

Quantum of Paperless

Partner's Guide to Accounting Firm Optimization

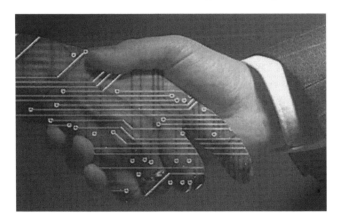

32 Quantum Leaps

To Improve Your

Accounting Firm's Productivity

Rosenberg Associates Edition

Quantum of Paperless

Partner's Guide to Accounting Firm Optimization

32 Quantum Leaps

To Improve Your

Accounting Firm's Productivity

Roman H. Kepczyk

Publisher: Roman H. Kepczyk
Phoenix, Arizona
United States of America

LIBRARY OF CONGRESS CONTROL NUMBER:
ISBN 1494983567

EAN-13 is 9781494983567

Printed in the United States of America by Create Space
Bulk purchases, please contact the author

Dedication

To Sylvie,

Stephan and Antoine,

and our Blessed Life

Table of Contents

Foreword by MARC ROSENBERG

How innovative are accounting firms?

This is a question I've had occasion to ponder lately, in preparation for speaking engagements at conferences and journal articles devoted to the future of the CPA profession.

I had some thoughts of my own, but as a long time pollster of the accounting profession, I knew that whatever I came up with must include input from great managing partners of CPA firms from coast to coast. The bulk of their responses indicated that over the past two decades change has been slow to come to a profession widely perceived as resistant to it.

Said Chris Fredriksen, Chairman/CEO of 2020Group USA:

> **"CPA firms tend to be reactive, late adopters and risk-averse. Shakespeare said, 'some are born innovative, some achieve innovation and others have innovation thrust upon them.' CPA firms are clearly in the last group," he stated, taking liberties with _Twelfth Night._**

However, the more I pored over my research, the more apparent it became that CPA firms are a lot more innovative than many of us think. Significant innovations that have occurred in the past 20 years or so convinced me that the profession has readily embraced an impressive list of changes.

Clearly, technology is THE major area of innovation for CPA firms. The way accountants do their work has been totally transformed and continues to change every year. Following are some major innovations Roman Kepczyk will address in this book:

1. Multiple screen/monitor displays – made possible a huge jump in individual productivity.

2. Smartphones and tablets, including the touch screen.

3. Cloud/SaaS including portals and addressing security issues.

4. Workflow, including paperless audit and other software and scanning technology.

5. Knowledge management.

6. Social networking –more an emerging technology because it has yet to have a big impact for CPA firms.

<u>How do top CPA firm managing partners ensure that computers and technology have the greatest possible impact on success and profitability?</u>

As a specialist in the overall management of CPA firms, I have a keen interest in how MPs perform their jobs. As is the case with most CEOs of sizeable organizations, the duties of a CPA firm managing partner encompass a long list of critical management functions. Certainly, one of them is ensuring that computers and technology are used in ways that have the greatest possible impact on firms' success and profitability.

To find out what MPs do to achieve this aspect of their job description, we polled a group of them from coast to coast.

RESULTS: 28 responses were received: 70% from firms with annual revenues of $5-15M, 20% from firms billing $15M and above, and 10% from $3-5M firms.

Detailed responses appear later in this forward. Here is an executive summary:

1. **Seek out national CPA industry technology experts.** This was the most often-cited technique practiced by our MP group. Veteran experts such as Roman Kepczyk and Randy Johnston provide a wealth of practical, hands-on experience because they work with dozens of firms each year and have done so for many years. In my field of practice management consulting, I tell my clients that I am one firm smarter than the last firm I worked with. Certainly, the same is true for these national IT experts. They learn from their experiences at other firms and are able to distill that knowledge into incredibly helpful advice and counsel to every new firm they consult with.

In addition to their experiences with firms, these consultants offer an objective view of your firm's IT functions. This is critical because IT directors tend to take a defensive view of their own operations and can be resistant to change.

2. **Make the IT director an integral part of the firm's management team**. Managing partners make sure to integrate IT directors into the vast majority of firms' management issues. It's critical for IT directors to have a firm-wide view on keeping all personnel working at the most efficient level possible.

   One takeaway from the above, that was not stated by our MP group, but certainly implied, is this: If your firm's IT director is not someone who is capable of performing as a vocal, credible and articulate member of the management team, then you probably don't have the right person on board for the job.

3. **Find ways to obtain the input of a good cross-section of firm personnel on the state and direction of the firm's technology.** Quite a few firms have formed IT committees, usually consisting of the firm administrator, IT director and younger partners with a high technology IQ. The committee is not so much a decision-making body as it is a think tank. It's also a great way to ensure that the IT director has input from a wide range of personnel.

4. **The importance of technology budgets.** MPs are heavily involved with their IT directors in the preparation of annual IT budgets to ensure that future needs are planned, anticipated and funded.

5. **IT directors need to interact with their peers.** MPs encourage their IT directors to venture outside the firm and observe how other firms of similar size address IT challenges. Whereas numerous peer networking opportunities exist for MPs, firm administrators and marketing directors, unfortunately, the same cannot be said for IT directors. So, it's incumbent upon either the MP or the IT director to initiate these networking opportunities with other firms, where none exist. Technology conferences and associations of CPA firms offer some great opportunities.

   For firms in larger cities, roundtable groups of IT directors from area firms that meet 4 to 6 times a year can be organized. I organized one in Chicago ten years ago that continues to meet to this day – and I'm not even an IT guy!

6. **Don't trust vendor sales people.** I love this one, even though only one person said it. This veteran MP of a very sizeable firm noted that canned demos are superficial and most of the sales personnel are not heavy-duty users of the product. The implication that I get from this tip is: Buy a technology based on the advice of credible, knowledgeable people who have successfully used it at their firms, not based on a touting sales person or an ad.

7. **MPs should acknowledge what they don't know and find ways to fill that knowledge gap.** Years ago, I worked with a dynamic, founding partner of a sizeable, hugely successful CPA firm. He was brilliant and super self-confident in his ability to run all aspects of a CPA firm…except computers and technology. He readily admitted this, and to combat this weakness, he was tenacious in his quest to seek the opinions of others who *were* knowledgeable.

   Techniques used by MPs to learn from others include:

   - Observe best IT practices from firms in their CPA firm association or roundtable group.
   - Get younger, technology-savvy partners involved in providing input to the firm's technology.
   - Make sure that the firm regularly gets input from the people in the trenches, the hard-core users of IT – the professional staff. Rely heavily on them.
   - National CPA firm IT consultants.

8. **Don't be stingy on IT spending**. MPs told us that good solutions cost money and time to do them right. Falling behind and losing production, they said, will cost your firm in the long run. Incidentally, this point about not being stingy does not mean that firms should be spendthrifts. MPs subject IT investments to a proper cost-benefit analysis, just as they do with any other major investment.

9. **Don't be an early adopter**. This suggestion was made by only one person, but I feel it is critically important. This piece of advice has been corroborated from my experience leading a roundtable group of IT directors for ten years and listening to them tell each other how they don't like to adopt first generation hardware advances and software releases. Let someone else debug them.

DETAILED RESPONSES

Numbers after statements represent the number of times people stating the item or something very similar. If there is no number after a statement, only one person said it.

Making the IT director an integral part of management

- Include IT directors on the firm's **management team** so they are integrated into all firm issues; meet with them often, and have them report on technology objectives at management meetings. We want them to take a firm-wide view on keeping our people working at the most efficient level possible. (7)

- Form an **IT committee** consisting of our firm administrator, IT manager and two younger partners to continuously evaluate our IT structure. (6)

- Hold continuous discussions with IT director **projecting future technology** needs and creation of **technology budgets**. As MP, I am very involved at a strategic level in planning our IT. (7)

- Get our IT personnel engaged in **benchmarking with other firms to discover best practices** and attending conferences. (5)

- Assign **IT director at least one effectiveness and efficiency goal** to drive our future productivity. One firm establishes a performance goal for their IT manager based on response rates from users. (2)

- Stress to IT personnel to **treat our employees as their clients**; to be the solution, not the problem. Our IT staff know that keeping the staff productive is most important. (2)

Usage of national IT consultants/experts

- Seek feedback and input from **CPA industry technology experts**. Regularly review our IT system by an external IT consultant. (9)

- **Don't expect objectivity from vendor sales people.** Their canned demos are superficial and most of them are not heavy-duty users of the product.

Learn from others; don't live in a cocoon

- Observe **best IT practices** from other firms in our **Association** and roundtable group. (6)

- Before implementing new software, we **test it out on one or two people** in our firm.

The MP's actions speak louder than words

- As MP, I act as a **role model** to all firm personnel, showing them how I personally utilize all aspects of our firm's technology to make me efficient. (2)

- **I listen to the staff** that use the technology and do the work. If they are frustrated or losing efficiency, then I need to respond quickly. They have greater knowledge of IT than I do. (4)

Maintain awareness of what is available in the marketplace. (4)

Overcome resistance to change by fully exploring new technologies. Continually play the devil's advocate with challenging why or why not. (2)

Stay current; ensure that wise decisions are made

- **Assign technology-literate partners** to coach our IT personnel and developing IT budget. (3)

- Don't be stingy on IT spending. Know it **won't be cheap.** Good solutions cost money and time to do it right. Falling behind and losing production will cost you in the long run. (2)

- **Don't be an early adopter**. Verify other firms' experiences before adopting something for us.

IT spending, budgeting

- Make sure there is a **cost-benefit analysis** to any proposed new IT investment. (2)

- Create a formal, written **hardware replacement program**. Insist on providing staff with the latest technology. (3)

Specific software

- Use **cloud computing** as much as possible. (4)

- **Go paperless;** use document management software. (2)

- Client **access to tax returns through secure portal**.

- Ensure that we have great **security** and reliable backup systems.

- Implementation of **CRM**.

- Improved financial **flash reports**.

- Make sure that technology is featured in our **intranet**.

Ensure efficiency of firm personnel, especially in the field

- Provide **remote work** capabilities for all staff. (3)

- We do lots of audits, so we make sure our auditors **take advantage of technology in the field** by carrying laptops less than 3 years old, scanners, extra monitors and high speed internet connections.

- We have a **process committee** that reviews project workflow. (2)

- All accountants use **laptops**, not desktops, to enable mobile computing.

IT training

- Include IT "basic **training" at staff meetings**. The biggest efficiency challenge is closing the knowledge gap between our team members – people can't improve if they don't know what they don't know.

- We put on periodic **lunch and learn programs** in various software programs.

Rosenberg's additions to the list

Make no bones about it. I am not an IT expert. Not even close. But I love technology, embrace it and am always asking MPs from CPA firms what they are doing to harness the power of technology. Although the items that follow are generally less important than those listed on the previous pages, nevertheless, there is value in these ideas.

IT Training. The lack of formal training that firms provide their staff in operating hardware and software is a pet peeve of mine that experts are at a loss to explain. Throughout this forward, we have discussed the immense impact of technology on how accounting firms do their work. But for some reason, firms are satisfied with pointing their personnel to computers and telling them to "figure it out." Oh sure, if the firm has a halfway decent new employee orientation program, and staff are courageous enough to ask for help from knowledgeable staff, people learn from watching others and eventually grasp what they need to know. But to me, this is a lousy way of ensuring that firm personnel learn to master technology.

Separate internal from external IT personnel (the latter are known as consultants). By now, we all agree that efficient technology is critically important. As we all know, the nature of computers is that problems, questions and changes arise on a regular basis. So, CPA firms need to have a cadre of people – let's call them internal IT personnel - who stand ready to support the rest of the firm as they use their computers.

Some firms, in a misguided effort to increase revenues and profits, use their internal IT people to do external consulting to clients. This is a huge mistake!

Take the case of your top IT person whose annual salary is $80,000 - $40 an hour. One day, the firm identifies a project for the IT person at a client, billed at a rate of $160 per hour. The project takes 50 hours, which results in a nice, tidy invoice to the super-pleased client of $8,000, at 100% realization. Well, the IT person isn't stupid. He compares the kudos and self-fulfillment of earning $8,000 for the firm vs. responding to a support call by Frank the Dumb CPA who barely knows how to turn his computer on. It's no contest. As more consulting projects come in (but not enough to justify making this a full time position), guess what most gets IT people most excited about their jobs?

It's only natural that the IT person's first priority will be consulting to clients, at the expense of giving world class service to his most important clients – the firm's personnel. Don't mix internal and external IT – it's a disaster waiting to happen.

Dashboards. Partners at CPA firms are extremely busy people. There are a lot of things that they need to keep track of – simultaneously:

- The status of 8 client projects, including how the actual time compares to budget.
- 14 client receivables that range from $5,000 to $20,000 and are all 120 days past due.
- 19 completed client projects that have yet to be billed.
- A stack of 4 workpaper files on completed projects that need to be reviewed.
- The lunch meeting at Rotary this afternoon.
- Follow-up phone calls to three prospects.
- Etc. Etc.

In an ideal world, all of the above should be monitored on a daily basis. But that's very difficult to do with traditional systems. Staying on top of key metrics and statistics is a lot easier with the use of a dashboard – a user interface that, somewhat similar an automobile's dashboard, organizes and summarizes information in a manner that is easy to read and updated on a real-time basis, thus making it easier for partners to keep current.

Work in Process. This is somewhat of a subset of the dashboard item above. One of the main reasons firms have WIP write-offs is that partners find it impossible to stay on top of all of their client projects that are simultaneously in progress. A write-off arises when, after a project has been completed, the partner finds out that $20,000 of time has been accumulated on a job quoted at $10,000. In almost all cases, it's too late to resolve the problem and the excess time is written off.

Perhaps if partners had been alerted of the *trend* of excess time being incurred *during the job*, before most of the excess time is incurred, they'd have been able to intervene and minimize the damage. The vast majority of CPA firms' systems do not provide partners with prompt notification of trends that will result in write-offs.

Email. The incredible time waster. Email hygiene at most firms stinks. Every day, it seems that we read about research showing the incredible amount of wasted hours spent on email. Who knows which study is accurate, but it's clear that, during the course of a year, dozens if not hundreds of hours are wasted. This is an easy fix, but firms usually adopt a "hands off" policy on monitoring how firm personnel use their email. The result of this neglect is lower productivity.

****

You are now ready to begin reading Roman's epic book, *Quantum of Paperless.* I have known Roman for 15 years or so and regard him as the nation's #1 CPA firm IT consultant. This high praise doesn't just come from me. More importantly, it comes from my clients, in two major ways.

First, I have referred Roman to over a dozen clients from coast to coast. All of them rave about Roman's work.

Second, I run three CPA firm practice management roundtable groups in Chicago, each with roughly 25 member firms. Roman has presented a special half-day workshop to the roundtable firms for the past several years. Though we get a few IT directors and firm administrators, the biggest attendance block consists of managing partners and client service partners. To me, this is testimony to Roman's unique ability to deliver leading edge, highly usable recommendations pitched at a level easily understood by partners lacking IT expertise. Not many IT consultants have this talent.

Here's a brief summary of the feedback we have received on Roman from these workshops:

- "Perfect"
- "Great session."
- "Excellent"
- "Roman is someone I learn from over and over again."
- "What he offers is uniquely valuable."
- "I always get new ideas to bring back to my firm."

When asked what attendees particularly liked, one person simply responded "Roman." Roman is the best and I am thrilled that he asked me to contribute to "*Quantum of Paperless.*"

Enjoy.

Marc Rosenberg, CPA

Forward by ROMAN KEPCZYK

Congratulations on your first step in taking control of your firm's future technology direction. Most Partners and Administrators who oversee the firm's technology decisions are already working full time at their existing responsibilities. They just don't have the time, energy, or internal resources to become experts with every aspect of firm production, let alone to research and decide on the broad range of optimum accounting technology solutions to implement.

This Guide is written specifically to help you understand:

- Today's thirty-two mission critical digital best practices that will push your firm forward with quantum leaps in productivity
- A structured process to prioritize those opportunities
- Solutions targeted to your firm and your clients.

Working under the premise of the Pareto Principal, the goal of this Guide is to expose you to the 80% of important firm optimization opportunities in a clear, condensed, and comprehensive format that will require 20% of your time to thoroughly identify and understand.

TO MAKE QUANTUM LEAPS IN YOUR FIRM'S PRODUCTIVITY:

1. Optimize your time by reading this Guide in one sitting, which should take between one and two hours.
2. Complete the Firm Optimization Checklist while you are reading and thoughts are fresh in your mind.
3. Put it away for a day and then re-evaluate your prioritization focusing on the top one to three initiatives in each area.
4. If other personnel can provide valuable input, have each individual read the Guide and complete their own Checklist.
5. Meet as a team to set priorities at a firm wide level.

As with all strategic initiatives, the key is to identify the most important firm opportunities and assign accountability to one person for that task, providing them the requisite personnel and resources to accomplish the task. It is always better to focus on one to three items through completion, rather than "wishful" thinking on a laundry list.

Overview

Every accounting firm is unique in the production processes they have developed over time to service clients, produce tax returns, complete audits, enter time, and produce billing. While each firm is unique, the transition from traditional manual processes to today's digital solutions is remarkably similar and it is primarily a matter of identifying where the firm is today and implementing the next proven process that firm personnel are sufficiently capable and willing to adopt.

This Guide is broken into 32 mission critical quantum leaps where your firm production can be optimized. In each section, proven solutions that accounting firms are successfully implementing and using today are listed. Where appropriate, the results of the Association for Accounting Administration's (CPAAdmin.org) 2015 Benchmarking Paperless Best Practices survey to support solutions utilized during the 2015 busy season are included. These can be found at the back of this Guide as well as at www.QuantumOfPaperless.com.

Implementing any one, or all of the solutions discussed will allow your firm to make Quantum Leaps towards optimizing your firm production this year.

Your Hardware

Talking about hardware may seem like an odd place to start a discussion on optimizing your firm production. However, without a solid framework in place to promote a stable working environment and take advantage of today's technologies, your firm's ability to effectively implement solutions will be severely restricted.

Pushing your IT infrastructure, which includes all of your file servers, cabling, applications, workstations, and Internet connectivity beyond basic limits will lead to more "dinking" time by your professional staff. *("Dinking" is the technical term for the massive amounts of time wasted by your personnel when computers lock up or don't do what is expected and when they have to "dink around" trying to figure out a solution).*

Even though people are an accounting firm's biggest asset, and consequently expense, very few firms effectively track the lost downtime caused by IT issues which usually ends up being buried within chargeable time to the client. The cost of your personnel's down time dwarfs the cost of having the proper IT infrastructure.

Remember, the sole purpose of your IT infrastructure is to enable people to convert information provided by clients into useful business products such as tax returns, audit reports or other financial reports as efficiently as possible. Therefore, the firm has to start with a solid core.

QL #1: Monitor Real Estate-More is Better

The best place to start the discussion on hardware is with monitors as it is the easiest place to see an immediate return on your IT investment. Your monitors are your windows into all digitally stored information and are the foundation for improving every aspect of firm production. Transitioning tax production processes from physical to digital requires that all input screens and

> *"80% of responding firms utilize more than two traditional monitors"*
> *-CPAFMA 2015 Paperless Benchmarking*

source documents be simultaneously viewable in a convenient format, which today means *more* screen real estate per workstation.

Dual monitors have been considered the standard in firms as far back as 2009 with many firms adding a 3rd or 4th monitor along with maintaining their older screens. The 2015 survey pointed to many firms replacing their older 17" and 19" screens with oversize monitors (28" or larger), effectively giving them triple/quadruple screen space. The survey found that this past busy season 55% of firms utilized triple monitors and 25% had gone beyond this with either quadruple monitors or dual oversize screens. An added benefit of using oversize dual screens is that that fit better into cubicle areas where there may be vertical space limitations due to built-in shelving.

Before firms can effectively transition to front end scanning or use digital workflow processes, they must have the additional screen space for tax personnel working in these applications. Often times, personnel ask why they just don't buy one huge 40" display screen and open multiple windows, and the main reasons are cost, screen clarity, and ergonomics. Today, it is less expensive for firms to add one or two high resolution 28" or larger monitors at a time than to jump to one oversize screen that has sufficient quality to be able to work for the long hours that tax season requires. Older monitors had resolutions of 1080p or less, and spreadsheets and images become less "crisp," as the screen becomes larger. Firms should be buying monitors with the highest "cost effective" resolutions (3K: 2880x1620 pixels and 4K: 3840x2160 pixels) as they will be using them for four or more years. Finally, sitting close to a single large flat screen is harder to view than multiple angled screens.

QL #1: Monitor Real Estate-More is Better

While ultra-high resolution "curved" displays were introduced in 2014, it will take a few years for the cost to come down enough to be economically feasible so most firms still purchase traditional flat screens. Windows 7 and 10 have made connecting multiple monitors easier than ever.

To begin, not all monitors are created equal. Today's standard is at least 20" and should be flex or "pivot" capable. This enables viewing in a vertical or "portrait" mode and horizontal or "landscape" mode. The CPAFMA 2015 survey found that 45% of responding firms utilized at least one monitor in a vertical mode. Seeing an entire scanned source document without scrolling or having to shrink the image into a smaller space, increases productivity immediately.

While it is easy to get users to dual screens by plugging an external monitor into the workstation's existing video port, getting to three or more screens requires additional video ports (DVI/HDMI/USB) and if not available, specialized hardware such as displays with integrated DisplayLink and DisplayPort video capabilities or in the case of older monitors, the use of external screen splitters. Dual oversize screens minimize the need for these additional hardware configurations and will be effective if the firm invests in ultra-high resolution monitors.

> **QL #1 ACTION:** Identify all tax professionals and document the number of oversize monitors that will be needed to bring all users up to the screen capacity of at least three monitors.

QL #2: Scanners: Capturing Source Documents

One of the keys to optimizing production processes is capturing information at its "root" source. This means when data *enters* your firm, regardless of the format (mail, fax, email, or on a flash drive). Ideally, documents would be provided to the firm in a digital format such as secured email or preferably through a web portal, but the reality today is that a significant portion of accounting firm source documents arrive from clients in a traditional paper format. Your firm will need to develop processes to efficiently scan, name and store these documents. This digital Quantum Leap process is discussed in more detail later. Having the right physical scanners in place is required to optimize the timely capturing of data at three levels: production, workgroup, and individual.

Production scanning needs to be a centralized process. As far back as the 2009 AAA survey, 81% of firms utilized administrative personnel to do this as it promotes standardization and captures documents at a lower cost, even if much of the scanning was done at the back end. The 2015 survey found that 75% had transitioned the scanning process to the front or mid-level such that preparation and review were being done onscreen, another key Quantum Leap process. The key to selecting a production scanner is to evaluate how easy it can integrate within your document management or tax workflow application.

Most of the traditional high end copier/duplicators scan all documents to a specific employee or network directory and some allow the files to be named at the time of scanning. While these devices are acceptable for workgroup scanning, they can be counter-productive for any volume scanning. Dedicated production scanners can handle a larger volume and do a better job of adapting to different sizes and colors of documents, which reduces the amount of rework.

To optimize scanning production, your administrative personnel need to be well trained on tax document organization and have a workspace where they can immediately review, organize, and save the source documents. This step requires using dedicated workstations attached directly to the production scanner. Today's standard scanners are Fujitsu

QL #2: Scanners: Capturing Source Documents

and Canon units that are capable of processing 50 pages per minute or more and utilize on-the-fly correction software which comes with the scanners, such as Kofax VRS (VirtualReScan) to further minimize manual handling. Throughout the office there also needs to be workgroup scanning capabilities for smaller jobs and most firms utilize their copier/duplicators for this purpose or purchase smaller multi-function units that can also print and copy, such as those by HP or Xerox, which scan at 30+ pages per minute.

Certain individuals on the audit team or within administration and marketing frequently receive physical documents that need to be scanned. Individual workstation scanners such as the Fujitsu ScanSnap iX500 are effective in addition to the workgroup brands described above. While the ScanSnap devices are not TWAIN compliant (can't print directly within audit binders), they are cost effective for documents to be archived or managed within the firm's audit document container. For TWAIN compliant scanners, Canon has their personal DR (C225) series that allow staff to scan directly to their audit engagement applications. Finally, for quick capture of a small number of documents, today's smartphones have extremely powerful cameras that allow an auditor to take a picture of a receipt, capture the text with optical character recognition and email it.

QL #2 ACTION: Purchase dedicated production scanners attached to workstations for administrative department to promote centralized scanning and train professional staff on utilizing workgroup and individual scanners for capturing physical paper documents.

QL #3: Desktops vs. Laptops

Getting the right mix of mobility is critical for firms today. The accounting professional's Rule of Thumb is that everyone who works out of the office one day per week or more and needs to be self-contained, should have a laptop as their only machine. The obvious exception to this is for tax or administrative personnel that would never work from remote client sites, but have a computer at home which they can use to connect to the firm via a secure remote access solution. The string of natural disasters over the past two decades and the transition to more cloud-based applications has led to some firms making the decision that ALL professional staff will utilize a laptop as their only workstation.

Laptops should be scheduled for replacement every three years, whereas desktops are often functional for a fourth year. In firms that utilize workstations only as "dumb terminals" via tools such as Citrix and Microsoft Remote Desktop Server (formerly Windows Terminal Server), the functioning life of a desktop computer can be five or more years.

Today, there is little benefit in purchasing off-brand computers, and most firms buy desktops from Dell, Lenovo, Toshiba and HP/Compaq. One of the keys for a stable environment is to buy the *business* versions rather than consumer units and to standardize on as few models as possible within the firm. Studies done in the past found that such standardization could reduce the total cost of ownership by 26% or more. Firms have also found that buying, rather than leasing makes more sense, as the firm can roll out replacement computers at their convenience, instead of being forced to complete a transition by a specific date to return the leased laptops.

The key component firms should be concerned about on workstations is RAM and the firm standard should be a minimum of 8Gb to optimize today's 64 bit computers which are needed to effectively handle more monitors and the latest Windows operating systems. While older Windows 32 bit versions cannot effectively access more than about 3Gb of RAM, 64 bit workstations with Windows 7 and greater can handle 128Gb or more RAM. Firms should also purchase workstations with a minimum of an Intel Core i5 processor and preferably a Core i7 for more advanced users.

QL #3: Desktops vs. Laptops

One of the significant changes in laptop design that occurred in 2012 was the rollout of Ultrabooks™ that are less than 1" thin, weigh less than three pounds and have a battery life of more than five hours. These highly mobile devices were designed to provide an alternative to the proliferation of tablets which many desktop users were acquiring to do work when away from their desk. While tablets (Apple iPad, Android,) have become incredibly valuable tools for "consuming" information, the majority of work performed by CPAs is still done on traditional desktop and laptop computers that have access to multiple screens and full size keyboards. Microsoft's Surface Pro units are a fully functioning hybrid between laptops and tablets, but the overall cost is higher than traditional laptops and peripherals, so adoption in CPA firms has been cautious.

QL #3 ACTION: Maintain laptop and desktop inventory to identify annual replacement requirements and purchase name brand business-class workstations in as large a lot as possible to promote standardization.

QL #4: Scheduled Server Replacement and the Cloud

In most firms, the traditional core computers used for operating all applications are internal File Servers. Down time for a day or two is a disaster. If an "out of service" stoppage stretches to a week or more, your partner income will suffer measurably. Simply put, mission critical servers utilized for tax, audit, time and billing, and email have, at most, an effective five-year life. After this time equipment becomes significantly more difficult to maintain, whether you have a warranty or not. Your IT personnel should plan the transition to a new server at least three months in advance of any change to allow for adequate installation and testing. They should also seriously evaluate web-based alternatives where available as the cost of the application and maintenance can be significantly less than the firm doing it themselves.

For any single mission critical server replacement such as email or time and billing, you will want to compare the cost of outsourcing that service to the Internet in a hosted environment, which is referred to today as "Cloud" Computing. Cloud computing consists of ASP's (application service providers), SaaS (Software as a Service), externally hosted Citrix/Remote Desktop Server and any other technology that allows a user with an Internet connection to work remotely via a website hosted by someone other than the firm. These external providers can host an application for a monthly cost that is often less than the cost of the firm purchasing a server and maintaining that application for the next five years. Microsoft's hosted Exchange and Office 365 are examples where firms can pay as little as $4/month to host an individual email account.

Web-based tax and accounting solutions will become more prominent within both the WoltersKluwer/CCH and Thomson Reuters/Creative Solutions applications, as well as hosting client accounting such as Intuit QuickBooks through their online service or hosted providers such as RightNetworks and Xcentric. While Thomson Reuters has hosted their Virtual Office applications for many years, CCH rolled out their SaaS Practice, Tax, Document Management, Portal and Workstream at the end of 2009, which is under the Axcess name. Many firms utilize a "best of breed" approach in selecting accounting applications and end up with a hybrid solution where the more cost effective cloud applications are

QL #4: Scheduled Server Replacement and the Cloud

utilized in addition to continuing the hosting of traditional applications. In recent years, firms began outsourcing more and more IT technical expertise to external providers, effectively reducing their internal IT staff, which has led to some choosing to outsource their entire IT infrastructure to colocation, "private cloud" providers such as Xcentric. Please note that web-based solutions should ONLY be considered for firms that have reliable and redundant Internet access so that they can continue to work in the event their primary Internet connection is out.

Beginning in 2008, many larger firms transitioned to a new environment referred to as *server virtualization* with products such as VMware or Microsoft Hyper-V which the 2015 CPAFMA survey found 64% of firms utilize today. In a nutshell, this technology combines the functionality of two or more servers onto singular "super" file servers that can host separate instances of each application simultaneously. This translates to measurably lower costs and maintenance time for the firm, assuming the integrator has experience with server virtualization and implementing accounting firm applications.

Experience is crucial to implementing a virtualized server environment properly the first time. Typically, firms partner with an external integrator to get the installation done correctly. If in a worst case scenario you cannot find an integrator that gives you a high degree of confidence in their ability to implement this environment, forget about virtualization and go with a traditional network environment where you have "one server for each service," but have an IT team that can support your network, (after of course considering those applications that are more cost-effective in a hosted/cloud environment)

The worst and most unreliable network installations consistently happen to firms where internal IT personnel convince partners they can "do it all themselves" when they have no prior experience or training on new applications or environments. The stakes of downtime in a CPA firm are too high so don't let your firm be a science project!

QL #4: Scheduled Server Replacement and the Cloud

QL #4 ACTION: Inventory file servers and identify projected replacement cycle considering opportunities to utilize web-based solutions or consolidate servers if experienced integrators are available. Outsource all "one shot" projects to integrators with depth of personnel and experience with multiple implementations after evaluating which applications are more appropriate in a hosted/cloud environment.

QL #5: Offsite Backup/Internet

Your firm's safety net in the event of ANY disaster is your data backup. It better be consistently performed and securely stored offsite. Typically, firms have a problem when the process they relied on to make the backups didn't work or the tapes weren't complete because all their data no longer fits onto one tape. This is becoming a common problem as more data and more applications add significantly more volume, making the backup application require more storage and a longer running time to complete.

> *"67% of firms backup all their data to the Internet with 56% doing so on a daily basis"- CPAFMA 2015 Survey*

When backups are run during normal business hours, it can slow down the entire network, impacting everyone's performance. Make a note that the tape drive you have today, will be the *last* one you will ever own.

Today's disk-based and Internet backup solutions can provide better reliability without relying on personnel to physically swap tapes. While larger firms will build storage area networks, this technology is often priced out of range for most small to medium size firms. The practical solution for a small firm is to have a very fast hard drive attached to the network that can make "snapshots" of the firm's data throughout the day, which can then be securely copied offsite via the Internet or backed up to a removable disk/tape separately.

These drives are typically referred to as SANs (Storage Area Networks) or for smaller backup needs, they are called Network Attached Storage (NAS). These devices can restore a lost or damaged file faster and easier than retrieving a tape from an offsite location, loading the index and then restoring the file. We recommend using the SAN/NAS disks as an intermediate step.

In the event of a disaster, you will need to have offsite backup. If your tape system is still effective and you have a process to move it offsite reliably on a daily basis, stick with that as long as it works and is cost effective (but make sure the data is verified and encrypted in the event the tape is lost or stolen). However, when the capacity of the data

QL #5: Offsite Backup/Internet

exceeds your tapes or if you have to purchase a large number of blank tapes, it will be time to compare the cost of using local disk backups and an Internet backup service to that of buying a replacement tape drive. The hidden costs in tape drives are not only the new hardware, updated software, and stack of 30+ blank tapes, but also the administrative time swapping the tapes and transporting them offsite.

Archiving to a local SAN/NAS hard disk array and then having that device backed up offsite is becoming the standard for data backup.

As the cost of reliable broadband Internet access and offsite disk storage space has been driven down over the past few years, more firms are finding that there are web-based backup solutions that are cheaper, more reliable, and can run on an automated schedule. Individuals and small firms can utilize hosted services such as McAfee Online Backup, SOS Online Backup, EVault, Mozy Pro or Carbonite, whereas medium to larger firms will want to manage their own offsite backups themselves using tools such as Datto, Veeam, Dell AppAssure and EMC Data Domain which can back up to a storage device either in another of the firm's locations or to a custom hosted co-location facility.

Firm's today should look for providers that have experience with accounting applications and can virtually rebuild the network or create a private cloud in the event of a disaster, which should become an integral part of the firm's disaster recovery plan. The beauty of these Internet-based services is that they can be set to backup automatically every few minutes and keep any number of versions in a secure offsite location, Thus the firm has the ability to recover from any disaster and also get access to previous versions of a document if a file was accidentally overwritten "sometime in the last year."

> **QL#5 ACTION:** Have your personnel verify that ALL data is being backed up, verified, and stored offsite on at least a daily basis and that at least one person from *each* department is knowledgeable on how to find and restore a file. Ensure that all media that is moved physically offsite is encrypted to be in compliance with your State's cyber security laws.

QL #6: Windows 7 to 10 Transition

Okay, we all know that the Windows operating system is preferred to run computers by the primary vendors to the accounting profession. All decisions about operating systems have to be done carefully as it impacts software and hardware decisions for at least 3 – 5 years. While we don't place too much emphasis on the workstation operating system, one significant issue you can't overlook is increasing computer memory to function optimally with today's multi-monitor requirements and the multitude of concurrent applications your staff will be running. The key to operating systems is stability and the major accounting vendors (CCH, Thomson Reuters, and Intuit) preferred Windows XP through the end of 2009, at which time Windows 7 32 bit became the predominant product for purposes of optimal stability, which is acceptable for most audit and administrative personnel. However, for tax personnel with three or more monitors and the propensity to run many more applications concurrently, additional RAM is highly recommended. For this reason, many firms transitioned to the 64 bit version of Windows 7 with all new computer purchases as the optimal heavy production workstation standard through the end of 2014.

With Microsoft discontinuing support of Windows XP in April 2014, Windows 7 became the most prevalent operating system utilized within CPA firms, particularly as the initial release of Windows 8 received very poor reviews from CPAs (causing IT personnel to buy new computers and "downgrade" them to Windows 7). In 2015, Microsoft released Windows 10 (the Window 9 name was skipped) with the intention of having the same operating system running on accountant's workstations, tablets and smartphones. This is expected to reduce firm training and support requirements and make applications available across all devices.

To transition firms to Windows 10, Microsoft is offering a FREE upgrade to all licensed Windows 7/8 users through July 28, 2016 with the license being good for the life of that machine. We recommend firms pilot the upgrade after April 15, 2016 with the intention of upgrading all workstations that have adequate processor and disk capacity before the upgrade offers expire.

QL #6: Windows 7 To 10 Transition

We recommend all new workstations be purchased with Windows 10, i5/i7 processors, solid state disk drives and a minimum of 8Gb RAM for audit/administrative personnel and 16Gb RAM for tax personnel. It is anticipated that all software vendors will go with annual subscription pricing for all applications, including Microsoft Windows, Office, Adobe, etc.

QL #6 ACTION: Standardize purchases of new computers on Windows 10 for firm stability and verify all workstations have adequate RAM to handle multiple monitors and applications.

QL #7: Microsoft Office 201x vs. Office 365

To be effective in business today, every member of your firm must optimally utilize the Microsoft Office suite at an intermediate to advanced level for Outlook, Excel, and Word. Due to the lag of accounting vendors providing support to the latest versions of office, today's recommended standard is Office 2013. Many firms continue to utilize Office 2010 because some accounting applications (engagement binders) did not support Office 2013 until this past year. Firms should review their listing of accounting applications after the busy season to determine if they can transition to Office 2013 and the cost to do so, considering that Office 2016 has been out since September 2015 and will most likely be supported by the major accounting vendors in late 2016.

The latest Office applications promote efficiency through a standardized "ribbon" menu which takes advantage of today's wider screens and utilize symbols instead of pull down menus that use descriptions in words as well as a consistent outlay when utilized on a desktop, tablet, or smartphone. People see and react to images much quicker than they read words, which makes them more efficient. When one of the Office applications is learned, users are more proficient with all of them. As mentioned above, the top accounting vendors have worked out most of the bugs between their applications and the 2013 version of Office. If your firm is on Office versions 2007 or older, or has Microsoft Software Assurance where the upgrade is included, it is recommended that the firm jump to the 2013 version or consider the cloud-based Office 365 license that also includes local copies on your hard drive.

While many firms have transitioned to Office 365 for Outlook/Skype for Business, we recommend firms proceed cautiously for Word, Excel, and other productivity applications as the automatic Microsoft upgrades may be incompatible with the capabilities of your accounting applications, which traditionally take between 6-12 months to be supported. Always be sure to verify the compatibility of your specific applications with Office before upgrading!

Once you get the go ahead to upgrade to a new version, send some of your best communicators to advanced Excel, Word and Outlook training, so they can understand the improvements and then set up customized,

QL #7 Microsoft Office 201x vs. Office 365

accounting firm specific training for the rest of your personnel. While there are excellent web resources for training including Lynda.com, one exceptional training resource that works directly with many State CPA Societies is K2 Enterprises (K2E.com) that has very effective instructors and strong content tailored to accounting firm needs.

QL #7 ACTION: Verify the firm's audit/accounting applications are supported on the current Microsoft Office version and plan transition and training to one common version as part of firmwide roll out.

QL #8: Proactively Managed Application Updates

Every firm has concerns about their systems being hacked or getting attacked by a virus or malware. The 2016 CPAFMA IT survey found that 15% of firms had been infected with malware that caused significant downtime in the past twelve months. The vast majority of issues can be effectively negated with one simple process: *KEEP YOUR SOFTWARE UPDATED*. For workstations, your antivirus software should regularly look for updates and automatically install them. Microsoft Windows has an update feature that can be set to automatic for security upgrades. Turn them on and schedule them to run automatically, either overnight or on weekends.

On the server level, there is a slight twist to this issue. Oftentimes tax, audit and accounting applications are behind on their compatibility testing with new server versions. To combat this, it is always recommended that your IT personnel be onsite to run the updates on the servers, so they can roll them back if necessary. We recommend firms utilize the Microsoft Windows Server Update Services (WSUS) to automatically download the updates and then notify your IT personnel so they can manage the updates. Firms lose significant time to virus and other malware infestations, so regularly updated applications help sustain the firm's overall productivity.

Proactively updating applications so that everyone is operating on the same version also reduces conflicts which can occur when personnel have different versions running on their local workstations. Using network applications can alleviate this but requires firm personnel to run updates at their convenience. One advantage of utilizing today's cloud applications is that all updates are done by the vendor during scheduled maintenance windows which are usually performed late at night to minimize the impact on professional staff during working hours.

> **QL #8 ACTION:** Standardize procedures to verify that all workstation and server security updates are automated and completed on a timely basis.

QL #9: Remote Access Technology

Give your people access to the firm application and data resources needed whenever and wherever they are. They will get more work done in less time. One of the key components in optimizing firm production is providing the capability for firm personnel to work from anyplace, at any time, at their own convenience. Desktop users in small firms can get by with remote control tools such as GoToMyPC, LogMeIn,

> *"77% of firms stated they implemented remote access technology to access firm resources when away from the office."* - CPAFMA 2015 Survey

Join.me, or Windows Remote Desktop, which allows connection to their own desktop computer via an Internet attached workstation. However, for laptop users or personnel working in satellite offices, a more robust solution is needed.

If the firm has ten or more personnel that want to work concurrently from external sites, it becomes more cost effective to utilize a remote access server solution such as Citrix or Windows Remote Desktop Server (RDS formerly Terminal Server/WTS) or transition to cloud-based applications. Citrix and RDS servers act like a mainframe computer that connects to the firm's network and allows remote personnel to work effectively over slower Internet connections, even on older computers.

Remote workstations are setup as "dumb" computer terminals that only show screens and send keystrokes, and in most cases allow access to applications via a tablet or smartphone as well. The advantage to this technology is that once the remote user has gone through security screens to access the system, all work is done within the firm's secured network. In this way, there is little need for remote maintenance or support at the remote sites, and the risk of losing data is minimized. Today, a single remote access server can effectively handle approximately 18 concurrent connections and additional servers can be easily added (if planned for up front) for virtually any number of users.

For firms that have a satellite office with less than five users and very strong Internet bandwidth (1.5Mbps or more each way), an additional

QL #9: Remote Access Technology

option may be a Virtual Private Network (VPN). This technology extends the network connection from the main office to the remote site by using the Internet and securely encrypting all communications.

While the VPN process requires significantly more bandwidth than the above mentioned solutions, there are instances for a smaller number of users where VPN technology can be more cost-effective and easier to use than the remote server solutions. This question should always be asked of your Internet Service Provider before changing bandwidth solutions or deciding on a remote access strategy as different cable and fiber solutions can provide significantly different quality of service.

Once again, the advent of cloud applications allows users to work remotely on any Internet-enabled device, which includes not only remote workstations, but also today's tablets and smartphones. Firms should evaluate the overall cost of building remote access capabilities into their own network infrastructure against the use of cloud based applications. Firm's should also factor in the benefits of extending remote access to tablets and smartphones, which may be more convenient when away from the office, but should also be secured with today's mobile device management (MDM) applications. Apple iPads initially inundated the tablet category for accountants; many of these original units are becoming less effective with the larger operating system and application requirements that are standard today prompting accountants to replace them. In addition to iPads, firms should consider Android tablets, and even Microsoft's Surface device which are suitable solution for accountants.

QL #9 ACTION: Identify the number of personnel that will work out of the office one day per week or more. Determine the expected number of concurrent users within the next two years so that you can implement the appropriate solution today including use of tablets and smartphones for remote access.

QL #10: Internet Bandwidth

The Internet has undoubtedly had a profound impact on firm communications. It has become the primary driver towards the next generation of accounting applications that run entirely on the web through "cloud" computing. Before we get ahead of ourselves discussing cloud opportunities, we have to assess how the Internet is used within your firm today. Most likely the Internet is a digital pipeline, a conduit for communications, updates, research, and backups, and a platform for exchanging files with clients.

As a primary connection to the rest of the world, it is critical that firms have adequate bandwidth to handle the anticipated data transfer and communication volume over the next several years. In addition, it is important to have an alternative Internet connection available in the event that the primary connection is lost and not recoverable quickly.

The first major recommendation here is that firms proactively evaluate their Internet connectivity every 18-24 months. This is the usual timeframe for new providers to enter the market and/or double the available bandwidth through better technology and more competition. There can be a real opportunity to cut your monthly costs significantly. Reminders should be placed on your calendar at least six months before your contract renewal date so any changes can be installed in time for the usual two-year contract expiration.

Our second major recommendation in this area is get a secondary, *redundant* Internet connection on a different network backbone so that your firm will still have Internet access if the primary connection becomes unavailable. This usually means a combination of two of the following solutions: Metro fiber/MPLS, leased lines (T-1), DSL, cable, and wireless options. Internet access is completely dependent on what is available in your region, and specifically to what service is running down your street and can be connected into your office. Please note that the alternate connection today can also be a wireless solution such as city-wide Wi-Fi and WiMax providers, and the 4G digital cellular services are becoming cost effective for a small number of users. Firms should also re-evaluate their digital cellular contracts at least every other year as

QL #10: Internet Bandwidth

the major vendors rolled out "combined contracts" early in 2013 that would allow firm members to "share" data plans rather than have each person purchase bandwidth individually, some with unlimited data contracts. Areas with expensive local Internet cost attracts competitive solutions, which is why we recommend your firm review provider availability and pricing so frequently. To optimize the use of the redundant connection, firms should install dual-broadband capable routers, which connect both lines simultaneously and automatically failover (re-route) Internet traffic when needed. In this way, users are always connected.

QL #10 ACTION: Implement dual Internet connections with different providers and re-negotiate your contract for bandwidth and pricing every 18-24 months.

QL #11: Wireless Broadband Access

One of the revolutions in remote connectivity is happening within your cell phone, as digital cellular providers have beefed up and expanded their networks to provide reliable Internet access to remote devices. Today, the vast majority of the US and Canada has access to the Internet through the 4G digital cellular network at speeds of 1Mpbs or more, which is adequate for remote access to most applications, particularly those hosted by cloud providers.

"The AAA 2013 survey found that 94% of firms utilized smart phones for access to email, calendar and contacts. This was followed up in the CPAFMA 2015 survey which found that 54% provide tablets or netbooks to senior management"- CPAFMA 2015 Survey

The key today is to determine which service is the best in your firm's specific area of operations. Once you have determined the optimal cellular provider where you work, you can connect laptops, tablets and smartphones to the Internet via an integrated or external cellular hotspot," or by "tethering" a smart phone with shared Internet access. Laptops can come with an integrated wireless access option when you order them, but the recommended solution today is to utilize a mobile hotspot or the phone's integrated hotspot capability. While many firms provide a stipend to owners and managers to cover their mobile data plan, this is not as prevalent with staff where a shared Mobile hotspot such as the MiFi mobile hotspot devices which can be shared by five or more personnel in the field and utilize the 4G/3G networks.

QL #11 ACTION: Evaluate the best vendor in your region of operations and use a digital cellular connection either through an external MiFi device or smartphone "hotspot."

QL #12: Digital Communications: Unified Messaging

We mentioned in QL #1 that firms should strive to capture all data in a digital format at its "root" source. This goes for services such as the firm's fax and voice mail systems as well. Traditional inbound faxes are usually printed from a fax machine and then hand delivered to the recipient's desk. In some cases, this image is actually rescanned and emailed to the recipient. While this is a step towards digital delivery, today's digital fax systems deliver a digital image to the recipient via email so they can access them within their email.

> *"62% of firms utilize Unified Messaging technology for all staff and 54% of respondents use video/conference calling." - CPAFMA 2015 Survey*

Higher end copier/duplicators have integrated fax cards that will deliver the image to a designated administrative person who can update the subject and forward the fax to the intended recipient. For after-hours delivery of faxes, these systems can publish the fax to a public folder in Outlook or on a network drive that all authorized firm members can access (the same as a printed fax in the fax machine). If the firm's equipment does not have an integrated fax card, this can be either placed in a firm server using GFI FaxMaker or Castelle FaxPress for internal management, or outsourced to a hosted service provider such as Nextiva or eFax.

Firms should also consider the benefits of delivering voice messages through the email system, rather than having a separate system. Most of today's phone systems have the ability to transform a voice mail message into a .wav file that can be listened to on the recipient's computer, forwarded to others, and even saved in the firm's client file. The advantage to this is that end users consolidate ALL firm communications (email, fax, voicemail) in one place that can be made accessible through the Internet from any web-connected console.

Digital communications within firms is expanding to also incorporate video calling, screen sharing, file sharing, and integrated instant messaging, which are known as collaboration suites. The 2015 CPAFMA survey found that 47% had implemented a collaboration tool with instant messaging and 54% had implemented video calling. Microsoft's free Skype service is the most prevalent individual video

QL #12: Digital Communications: Unified Messaging

calling system used by firms and it is recommended that every firm have at least one video calling account setup and personnel trained on using it for when a client asks. Microsoft announced in 2014 that they will rebrand their Lync/Office Communicators tool to "Skype for Business" which is expected to be part of the overall Microsoft Office suite that CPA firms utilize. Unified messaging will eventually bring ALL firm communications to one platform so it is important to highlight that proper access security and awareness must be in place. By having all firm communications in one location it will be easier for your IT personnel (or a cloud provider) to do comprehensive backups and provide better security for all firm communications.

QL #12A ACTION: Capture faxes and voicemail digitally at the root source and make available securely in Outlook via the Internet.

QL #12B ACTION: Implement collaboration tools and train personnel on use.

QL #13: Capture Firm Knowledge

Firm knowledge and information is usually stored in one of four "buckets." The most obvious is within the accounting applications themselves where tax, audit and accounting programs store client files in a format that can only be accessed with that program. Files are usually indexed and accessed in designated directories so there is not much the firm can do about moving these files.

> *"72% of firms utilized an intranet to store firm wide information and 42% had a Microsoft SharePoint or Lotus Notes server knowledgebase."*
> *- CPAFMA 2015 Survey*

The second bucket for more advanced firms is a document management application where final documents can be archived in alignment with a comprehensive document retention plan and easily searched (Discussed in QL#14).

The third bucket is the network drive where the firm's client and administrative files reside. This is usually maintained with Microsoft Windows Explorer allowing anyone to create, move, and delete any files or directories. Unfortunately, this is often where the firm's core knowledge in the form of documented processes, procedure manuals, and administrative tools/forms reside. Accessing this knowledge requires lengthy searches and knowing exactly what the user is looking for.

To solve this issue, many firms have setup intranets to capture firm knowledge, which is the fourth information bucket found in firms today. An intranet is an internal website that uses Internet protocols to securely share the organization's information. It is only available to members of the firm who have authorized access. Many firms have developed intranets, because they have a familiar web interface, which is the most common method for searching information. However, the benefit of the intranet is that it can be easily customized and limited to firm members so they can search for specific items within the firm's policy manual, look up the firm's updated audit schedule, and access any personnel forms in one place.

QL #13: Capture Firm Knowledge

Traditionally, larger firms built their original intranets with Lotus Notes. Today, most intranets are developed with Microsoft tools such as Microsoft Expression, SharePoint and recently low cost cloud solutions such as WordPress and Intranets.com. Microsoft tools use similar menu structures as other Microsoft applications (Word, Excel) so it is easier to train administrative personnel to manage updates once the design is complete. All firm documents and knowledge that needs to be shared should be accessible through the firm's intranet.

Please note that the intranet industry is in a transition from traditional web design tools to more robust applications such as Microsoft SharePoint, which the CPAFMA 2015 survey found 42% of respondents were using. Most web design tools are extremely robust, but complex (and expensive) to use. Going forward, we believe most firms have opted to begin intranet design work with basic web design tools such as Expression and then transition those implementations into SharePoint or a more robust document management system when more features are needed.

There is also a trend amongst the practice management application providers to include "dashboards" into their products that display real time production metrics within the firm. These dashboards can be customized to each person's preference to highlight the key performance indicators (KPI) that they use to track their business and one-third of the respondents utilized information dashboards within practice management for internal reporting.

> *"33% of respondents utilized information dashboards within practice management for internal reporting"- CPAFMA 2015 Survey*

QL #13 ACTION: Setup firm intranet to host firm knowledge and resources that are not part of a production application or document management system and add dashboard products to monitor KPIs.

QL #14: Document Management

As discussed in the previous section, the network drive in most firms is not very well organized and requires the most cleanup. This happens because it is usually managed with Microsoft Windows Explorer, which allows almost anyone to create or access a file anywhere on the drive.

Unfortunately, there is seldom a firm standard that is adhered to, allowing users to create files with any naming convention they want and store it anywhere they please. The result can be files that are hard to find and slow to search across the network.

> *"78% of firms utilized a firm wide document management system"- CPAFMA 2015 Survey*

When we analyze firms, we find that there is a significant amount of redundancy in files, with multiple versions on network drives. These drives need significant clean up. While a solution would be to open every file, compare it to other versions, verify its contents and naming criteria, the time to do this for all documents is not practical. So the solution for managing documents in a paperless environment is to use a tool that will force adherence to the firm's document retention standards. This is done best by a document management system, which the CPAFMA Paperless survey found that more than three-fourths of firms had already implemented.

Document management systems come in a couple of levels with the most simple being "flat file" databases such as Thomson Reuters' File Cabinet Solution and Lacerte DMS, which create an index to quickly find files. These are very cost effective tools for firms to get started with and support firm standards for file naming conventions and directory structures so they are recommended over using Windows Explorer, even if just used for a couple of years with the intent of going to a more robust solution at a later time. While flat file solutions are effective for small to medium size firms, file access speeds can eventually slow down beyond the point of annoyance, as the size and number of files increases.

The next level would be the more robust databases such at CCH Document, Conarc iChannel, Doc-IT, and Thomson Reuters GoFileRoom that run on much more robust (SQL server) platforms.

QL #14: Document Management

These tools are significantly more expensive to implement but usually provide better performance for medium to larger size firms as well as more robust features for document search, retrieval and retention. These products usually have an integrated portal to transfer files to and from a client as well as more sophisticated audit trails to help with version control and determine who is authorized to access a specific file. Firms need to be serious about implementing and adhering to a document retention policy which is covered in QL #15.

While Thomson Reuters GoFileRoom started the trend towards cloud-based document management for accounting firms, CCH has responded with their Axcess Document Management tool and other smaller vendors such as SmartVault are optimizing their solutions for the accounting profession. Some advantages to consider for cloud-based document management systems is that the provider is responsible for all backups, disaster recovery, updates and expansion of space, which can quickly become a burden when smaller firms want to upgrade.

QL #14 ACTION: Transition firm files to a document management application.

QL #15: Document Retention Policy and Accountability

Managing digital files is in many ways similar to managing paper files in that the firm must have standards for who can create a document, add to or edit a document, file it, and eventually purge the file. Unfortunately, as digital files are on the network and "out of sight," many firms are not really aware of what files are stored, the most current versions and whether or not they should be deleted.

> *"71% of firms had an electronic document destruction procedure"- CPAFMA 2015 Survey*

As firms transition to the "less-paper" environment, it is critical that they implement a digital document retention policy and make users accountable for adhering to this policy. Microsoft Windows Explorer is one of the weakest and least reliable document retention solutions as virtually anyone on the network can create, edit, overwrite or even delete any document without recourse. Firms won't know a file has been damaged or destroyed until the point at which they can't find it or try to load it, which can be days, weeks, or even years after the change, and obviously too late. On the flip side, not having good naming conventions and directory structures can result in multiple versions of the same document leading to confusion and errors as to which document should be used, further wasting professional time.

The solution to this is developing a digital document retention policy and training personnel on adhering to firm standards. Ideally, firms will use a dedicated document management system that has an integrated or forced retention policy. This means that based on the document's profile, it would be flagged for deletion at its expiration date. The firm would have the option to keep or delete the file. This is much better than the current situation where someone would have to access and evaluate every file to determine what should be done with it.

QL #15A ACTION: Update firm document retention policy to include electronic documents and remind all personnel on firm retention policies.

QL #15B ACTION: Evaluate firm's document retention cycle and promote accountability for cleaning out obsolete files.

QL #16: Digital Tax Workflow System

The most important aspect of transitioning the firm's tax process to a digital environment is managing electronic files that are no longer physically viewable in assorted stacks around the office. This requires a digital tax workflow system that lets everyone know the status of every return and easily connects that person to digital copies of the return and the source documents. Under traditional manual tax systems, firms utilized due date tracking databases that identified when a return was due, but not what information was missing, or the preparation, review or extension status.

> *"59% of firms had implemented a digital workflow tool."* -2015 CPAFMA Survey

Many firms attempted to setup each of these statuses within their practice management systems via projects. It was soon discovered that in most firms, administrative personnel were the only ones updating the status when information was received and when the return went out. Those steps that were to be updated by the professional staff might be updated early in busy season, but compliance dropped off significantly the further along tax season went as they were not forced to update the status by the system. This usually resulted in many professional staff keeping their own manual lists or spreadsheets which doubled the work, and firms having weekly staff meetings to update the various workflow lists.

Some applications such as Lacerte integrate the workflow steps into their tax programs which can work well if properly utilized. Typically, most firms did not have this option available, which led to development of a new breed of workflow application that tracks the due date status, monitors the volume of returns at each status and assigned to each person, tracks any preparer or tax production notes, and integrates with email to improve communications. This information is attached to specific source documents that support easy access to all tax return information.

QL #16: Digital Tax Workflow System

Firms with a functioning document management system typically use an integrated workflow tool. Examples are Thomson GoFileRoom FirmFlow, CCH Workstream, OfficeTools Workspace, and Doc-It Workflow Manager. Integrated tools require less training and are often delivered at a lower cost than standalone tools.

Firms without a document management system can explore a range of workflow tools. Three of the most notable are Drake GruntWorx, SurePrep, and XCM Solutions. While SurePrep integrates workflow with their bookmarking and outsourced tax processing, XCM and GruntWorx are a web-based workflow system designed specifically for accounting firms. XCM can be integrated with either CCH Document Management or Microsoft Windows Explorer for managing digital tax returns and client source documents whereas CCH's Workstream is integrated with their latest Axcess Tax, Practice and Document Management products. We believe that these workflow tools are THE key to successfully managing today's digital practices and help facilitate effective front end scanning and digital tax optimization processes.

QL #16 ACTION: Implement a digital workflow system to track due dates, status of returns, staffing on projects and links to source documents.

QL #17: Optimum Scanning Applications/Procedures

For the next few years it is anticipated that accounting firm clients will deliver the majority of their organizers and supporting tax documents to the firm in a physical format. To utilize this information in a paperless environment, it must be effectively scanned and managed at the lowest possible cost. Early paperless adopters scanned the tax return and the supporting documents at the back end of the process when a return was complete. This is still usually the first step when firms transition from a completely manual environment. By doing backend scanning first, the firm can get used to working with digital files and naming conventions, prior to forcing changes in the preparation and review processes, which can then be transitioned to front-end scanning.

> As far back as 2009, the AAA survey found "86% of firms were scanning client supplied information and 81% were primarily utilizing administrative personnel to do the scanning" - 2009 AAA Survey

Scanning should be done primarily by administrative personnel (81% according to the 2009 AAA Benchmark Survey) to promote adherence to firm standards and so it is done at a lower cost. As mentioned in QL#2, firms have found that having a dedicated scanner attached to a workstation is the most effective method of capturing these images. The top rated scanners by firms who use them are the Fujitsu fi and Canon DR series. Images should be scanned at a standard 300dpi in black and white format. To minimize the amount of rescanning due to scan errors, firms should implement automatic correction software such as Kofax VRS, which does contrast resolution, de-speckling, and straightening on each image individually.

Once a firm has effectively implemented back end scanning, triple and oversize monitors, and a workflow tool, the firm can then consider mid-level or preferably front end scanning. Mid-level scanning integrates the traditional manual preparation process with files being scanned prior to review. The advantage to this process is that the tax review can be done anywhere and at any time the reviewer has digital access to the files. The other, preferred option is to go directly to front end scanning where

QL #17: Optimum Scanning Applications/Procedures

there are significant advantages for capturing and organizing information and eventually automatically inputting this data into the return.

Front end scanning can be optimized with a standard bookmarking application that takes the information provided by clients and electronically organizes it in a firm standard format. The resulting image file is in a standard PDF format which the preparer would have on one screen, with the tax input application on the other. Tools such as CCH FxScan, Thomson Source Document Scanning, and Drake Gruntworx can usually identify and organize between 50% and 75% of the client source documents. Therefore, the preparer would only have to move the remaining unidentified documents. For marking up these documents, many firms use Adobe Acrobat tools which can be somewhat cumbersome to use. More commonly firms use tools such as CCH PDFlyer, cPaperless TicTie Calculate, and XCM Solution's Toolbar which are extremely robust PDF annotation tools designed for accountants to add tic marks and calculator tapes (as well as using the Moffsoft Calculator for this purpose).

> *"70% of firms used digital tools to organize/bookmark scanned source documents and 47% are utilizing intelligent scanning tools that input data from the source document to the actual return"- CPAFMA 2015 Survey*

We believe all firms will standardize upon front end scanning processes within the next few years as they are the precursor to automatic input technologies utilizing optical character recognition. Today's scanning applications recognize many of the client's source documents for bookmarking along with the specific data fields from recognized forms. The application will place the data in the appropriate place on the tax return which CCH refers to as AutoFlow and Thomson Reuters calls Source Document Processing.

Additional features of the software include determining the level of accuracy of the scanned information and whether it is in the correct location if an error is detected, the application will change the color to

QL #17: Optimum Scanning Applications/Procedures

designate the error. This process will not only save time on the return preparation but also on the firm's review processes, which is often the most expensive bottleneck in the firm's tax production process.

QL #17: ACTION: Purchase adequate production scanner and implement scanning applications to organize and optimize the importing of tax information.

QL #18: Inbound Digital Transfer Tools

Again, one of the most critical steps in transitioning a firm to a "paperless" environment is capturing information in a digital format at its "root" source as that information enters the firm. At the base level, this means having clients provide you information in a digital format, which can be done via email, digital fax, or through a portal rather than with a physical document. While email is currently the most prevalent tool utilized by clients, it is anticipated the security concerns will help clients transition towards portals, which are discussed further in QL #26.

> *"82% of firms request audit documents prepared by clients be delivered in a digital format"- AAA 2013 Survey*

Email has been the most frequent tool used as most clients are comfortable attaching a spreadsheet or document and sending it to the firm. This method allows the digital file to be easily accessed and saved into the firm's file storage applications. While clients are usually comfortable with sending files to the firm via email, there are often times when the information is confidential. For privacy and confidentiality, firms need to use email passwords, email encryption, or a firm controlled portal. Applications that encrypt email such as CPA SafeMail and ZixCorp can be viable solutions. The cost of a secured connection with a client can be somewhat expensive, but can be justified for the firm's largest clients.

Fax machines are a second method of inbound delivery that clients will continue to use for a few more years because of ease of use which is discussed in more detail in QL#12. Traditional fax machines print out a physical document that is usually manually delivered to the recipient or scanned and attached to an email to be delivered electronically to that same recipient. Transitioning the process to keep the fax in a digital format that is linked to email when received will save on manual handling.

QL #18: Inbound Digital Transfer Tools

While email or a portal would be the preferred delivery solution, some clients will not have adequate Internet access and opt to bring in documents (such as their QuickBooks files) on a CD or USB Flash Drive. Firms should make a concerted effort to transfer this data to the network and return the media to the client immediately, so they are not tasked with disposing of the media.

The key to successful adoption of this Quantum Leap is to provide training and reminders to clients on how data should be transferred to the firm. Some firms have begun documenting this information on the firm's website as well as using remote screen control tools such as Join.me and LogMeIn to assist clients.

> **QL #18 ACTION:** Formalize process to have clients transfer files electronically.

QL #19: Firm Procedures Manuals

Every firm has accountants that are 10%, 20%, or even 50% more productive in their departments than other personnel because they have simply "figured it out." Unfortunately, when these people leave the firm, their unique knowledge of specific processes and short cuts goes with them. It is the responsibility of firms to capture these individuals' best practices so that their knowledge can be shared and accessed by all firm members both now and in the future. This can be accomplished by making a concerted effort to develop a best practices manual within each department.

The first step in the process is to lay out the production processes from start to finish on a flowchart, beginning with the first contact with the client through the billing of the service. Too many procedures manuals only deal with the specific application that is being utilized. The scope of the document needs to be expanded to identify and include every step in the firm's workflow including equipment and personnel.

The first step in developing a manual is for departmental personnel to accurately evaluate how well the firm performs each service activity and rating them by those:
- Done well and standardized
- Done well by some people but not standardized throughout
- Tasks that consistently cause problems and engagement overruns

The next step is to determine the processes where the firm would gain the most benefit from standardizing a specific process and identifying the individual who is best suited to set up and implement standards for that application. The firm would then allocate hours to that person on a weekly basis to work on identifying, documenting and educating firm members on best practices. As these people are usually the most effective (and requested) on their jobs, we suggest their time be limited to four hours per week on the project. Some firms have found that the most effective way to create standards is to break the effort into two focused two hour sessions each week for the specific purpose of documenting a best practice and educating staff on using it.

QL #19: Firm Procedures Manuals

During times when billable work slows down, the hours can be expanded and updated training scheduled. In this way, work gets done with minimal impact on each individual's week and the firm makes continual progress on capturing best practices.

QL #19 ACTION: Develop detailed departmental procedure manuals, update annually and provide ongoing training.

QL #20: Audit Field Equipment

The advent of today's audit "document container" applications has transitioned every aspect of audit production into a digital format. The key to successfully using these engagement applications is to make sure your personnel have the optimal equipment with them to work digitally. This includes multiple monitors, image capture equipment, and remote communications capabilities.

Firms have experienced how dual monitors improved overall productivity within the office and it is time for auditors to take that advantage into the field as well. According to the CPAFMA 2015 Paperless Benchmark Survey, 74% of firms were already carrying a second monitor in the field and it is expected that this

> *"74% of auditors are carrying dual monitors into the field"- CPAFMA 2015 Survey*

percentage will increase as accountants also use their tablets as an additional screen. As the tax department upgrades to triple or dual oversize monitors, older flat panel monitors are available for the audit team to take into the field or portable units such as Lenovo's LT1421, ASUS MB168B Plus and HP's U160 are utilized. Firm's should always pilot a mobile monitor before buying in volume as firms that purchased budget monitors in the past found them to have inadequate brightness options, be too bulky to transport, and have poor screen clarity.

While it is preferable to have clients transfer files electronically to the firm as outlined in QL#18, a number of supporting documents are not available to the auditor until they are onsite and meeting with the client. For those documents that are only in a physical format, the audit team should have access to a portable scanner that can capture images at a speed of at least ten pages per minute. Traditionally, firms have standardized on the Fujitsu ScanSnap iX series, which have been cost effective and portable. One problem is that the ScanSnap has not been "TWAIN" compliant. TWAIN capabilities allow a scanned image to be edited as a document rather than as an image and today's audit engagement binder tools can import TWAIN documents directly into the index.

QL #20: Audit Field Equipment

This has led a shift to firms either buying the more expensive Fujitsu fi series scanners or to other portable scanners such as the Canon DR series that are TWAIN compliant. Both scanners come with a full version of Adobe Acrobat which helps offset the cost of the scanner.

Finally, it is critical that firms provide Internet connectivity to all audit team members so that they can access firm resources, synchronize their audit binders, and enter time and expenses daily. Often, clients provide audit teams with a usable Internet connection. When clients provide access it is a good idea to outline the requirement parameters in the engagement letter. In any audit engagement of more than a few days, firms need to provide alternative access through the digital cellular networks if the client cannot provide usable access. Standalone mobile "hotspots" or those configured via today's smartphones provide Internet access at speeds from 100Kbps to well over 1Mbps, which is effective if the firm has remote access through a cloud based application, a direct link to their office workstation (via remote desktop access), or they can use a more robust solution such as Citrix or Remote Desktop Server for a larger number of users. Newer tools such as recent smart phone "hotspots" and the MiFi devices allow up to five auditors to share one connection as discussed in QL#11.

QL #20 ACTION: Outfit audit teams with appropriate digital tools and training to work effectively in the field.

QL #21: Audit Efficiency Training

Traditional audit practices use the previous year's audit programs and processes updated for the current year as their standard operating plan. Eventually this can lead to a significant amount of "over auditing." Breaking this habit is difficult as every level of staff has been trained in the manual processes and falls back on them when deadlines approach.

Many firms have rightfully transitioned to digital "document container" applications such as CaseWare, CCH Engagement and Thomson Reuters Engagement CS. Not all of these firms have changed their approach to reviewing progress on the audit and the financial reporting on a computer screen in a digital format. Using only the computer and digital files requires a radical change in every aspect of audit production and it is recommended that firms bring in someone from the outside to streamline audit production with digital tools. This can be accomplished by hiring a manager with extensive paperless auditing experience from another firm or using audit efficiency consulting organizations such as AuditWatch, AuditSense, and ACCOUNTability Plus.

These groups have documented best practices for every step of audit from the rollover of the previous year's financial reports through the digital delivery of the final report, all in an electronic format. Studies have shown firm's experiencing 10% or more increased productivity immediately, which usually covers the firm's initial investment. By documenting these procedures as part of the firm's departmental procedures manuals (QL#19) this information will be available to all new hires for training, as well as being made available to personnel in the field, which further promotes adherence to firm standards. These groups can also discuss the advantages of having work programs that integrate directly with the engagement applications. Both CCH and Thomson have made significant strides in integrating tools into a complete audit suite. Firm audit teams should compare the capabilities of Thomson's web-based AdvanceFlow audit container integrated with PPC Smart Practice Aids against CCH's Engagement binder with CCH KnowledgeCoach tools to see if a switch is warranted in 2016.

QL #21 ACTION: Hire formal digital audit efficiency organization and document processes within audit procedures manual.

QL #22: Daily Time/Expense Entry

Studies done over the past two decades have clearly shown that there is a significant improvement in realization for firms that enter, release, and post time and expenses on a daily basis. This process allows for daily or "hotel" type billing which is sent out with the completion of each billable project. The next step in the evolution of time and billing systems provided real time dashboards to report on firm activities and effectively allow firms to generate invoices. This can work *only* if all time and expenses for all personnel are captured within the system. While most firms have a daily time entry "policy" the biggest abusers of the policy are owners and managers, so it is about time for them to get onboard and use the system.

> *"67% of firms were preparing the majority of invoices onscreen rather than using manual billing sheets and 35% delivered invoices electronically."-CPAFMA 2015 Survey*

As we keep stating, all professional staff today have at least dual monitors and the majority have the screen real estate of three or more. This allows users to have their timesheet open at all times and enter information throughout the day, so that it can be reviewed and released before walking out the door. This will require training and some adjustment on the owner's part, but this is a first and most critical step when moving to daily billing and reporting. If management doesn't get onboard, they are wasting any investment in a new time and billing system. This choice can diminish the value of their practice.

Once everyone is onboard with "live" time and expense capture, the firm will be in a position to create an invoice with the completion of each project. These time capturing systems support both on screen entry and on screen invoice generation. With this information immediately available it is recommended that the "in-charge" for a client generates the invoice and the owner can then approve it on screen for administration to process. By doing daily billing, the majority of invoices will go out faster, improve the cash collection cycle and leave a smaller volume of traditional month end billing, mailing and paper sorting.

QL #22: Daily Time/Expense Entry

Today's time and billing systems can also generate invoices in a PDF (rather than physically printed) format. These can be emailed to the client as an attachment with or without password security. This significantly reduces the amount of administrative handling to print, stuff, and send the invoice, delivers it directly to the client within seconds, and creates an audit trail of when it was sent out. When properly configured, the invoice delivery process can be automated to save the PDF and attach it to an email or portal to be delivered to the client, which is today's recommended best practice.

> **QL #22 ACTION:** Mandate daily time entry, release and posting and provide training on daily billing processes.

QL #23: Digital Report Delivery

Improving firm efficiency means that the owners have to get onboard. One of the more obvious opportunities is the delivery of the firm's own financial reports. Many firms still print a hardcopy of the monthly financials and

> *"84% of firms delivered internal financial reports digitally"-* *CPAFMA 2015 Survey*

distribute them to each owner, many of whom physically store these documents in a binder or drawer in their office.

Most firms consider these documents confidential and yet copies are distributed throughout the office, many of which are not secured. A better solution is to set up an "owner's drawer" on the firm's portal or document management system and post ONE copy of the monthly financial statements when they are ready. Owners will be able to log in or click on a link in an email to get to the directory. With this method, all previous financial statements can be stored in one place for easy as needed access. This directory would also be securely backed up according to standard firm procedures.

A distinct advantage of digital files over paper files is that they can be accessed by all the firm owners at the same time via online means instead of having to come into the office to get the paper version. Another advantage of using the firm's own portal is that it will train owners to use the portal at least monthly, which will then make it easier to recommend for clients. Best practices in firms also target delivery of firm financial reports by the 10th of the month.

QL #23 ACTION: Standardize all firm financial reporting to digital format and electronic delivery/notification to all recipients.

QL #24: Online Banking/Remote Deposit

One of the easiest processes to convert to paperless with an immediate ROI is the firm's system for depositing client checks. Manually receiving and physically going to the bank to deposit checks can be time consuming and subject to too many errors. The manual procedure requires firms open mail on a daily basis, make copies to file in a binder, complete deposit slips and then send a person physically to the bank which can easily take a half hour every day, five days per week, fifty-two weeks per year.

> *"76% of firms utilized remote CheckScan for deposits" - CPAFMA 2015 Survey*

The solution today is using the bank's remote deposit system, that is often referred to as CheckScan which the CPAFMA 2015 Survey found was being utilized by 76% of firms. The bank provides the administrative department with a scanner that is securely connected to the bank via the Internet. The firm's administrative personnel scan the check, verify the information on the screen, and the bank prepares a digital deposit slip and stores this scanned document for the firm which can be accessed to record entries into the firm's accounting and practice management applications. The firm must dispose of the checks after 60 days, but the time traditionally spent on copying, filling out slips and going to the bank is eliminated.

Most banks today are *giving* the scanners to the firms and charging a nominal fee on a monthly basis as it reduces the banks needs for onsite tellers. For multi-office firms in rural areas, the outlying offices can utilize one central bank for deposits. The additional advantage of having this information online is that individuals that are authorized to access the account can see the deposits online and take advantage of online banking capabilities, which includes managing the firm's own sweep account and reviewing account transactions online. By reducing the amount of manual steps and doing more banking online, firms can further reduce their monthly bank service fees.

QL #24 ACTION: Setup online banking for daily account review and implement check scanning technology for daily remote deposit.

QL #25: Digital Accounts Payable Processing

Processing accounts payable is another of the manually intensive processes within the firm's administrative department that can be significantly streamlined through digital processes. Consider how many "touches" a single payable creates: receipt of the invoice, timing of payment in a folder, writing the check and attaching the stub, sending it to an owner for signature, filing a copy of check with backup in its own folder, and stuffing, sealing and sending the check to the vendor.

> *"52% of firms utilize credit cards and other electronic means to pay the majority of their invoices." - CPAFMA 2015 Survey*

Now imagine doing this a hundred times per month, every month. Imagine the volume of physical accounts payable vendor files both onsite and in storage, that can be eliminated by storing these images digitally.

The very simple solution is to pay as many recurring vendors as possible via a dedicated credit card and have them send you invoices via email. This credit card would be in the name of the owner signing the payables, but that owner would not get to use that card. Only the accounts payable person would have access to charge on this account so they can contact all vendors and put charges on automatic payment. When an invoice is emailed to the accounts payable person, they would enter the amount into the firm's accounting system on the date the item would be charged and save the invoice in a digital folder. By using a naming convention that would include the date of the entry and the vendor, the invoice would be easily accessible on the network (as well as being backed up).

When it is time to pay the credit card bill, the firm's controller will reconcile the account, review any questionable items onscreen, and then deliver the reconciled credit card statement to the owner for signature. A single payment can be made in lieu of all the individual checks. Many firms schedule large payments to hit after the credit card statement cutoff date to maximize the credit float and all of them use credit cards that earn "affinity" benefits. While airline miles and points were popular in the past, most firms are opting for maximum cash rebates, so the payables credit card is viewed as a firm discount program.

QL #25: Digital Accounts Payable Processing

For those vendors that will not accept credit card payments, the process can still be automated digitally. Most banks have digital bill payment systems and Bill.com is a web-based vendor that will route invoices electronically for approval and deliver the check through mail or electronic transfer for the firm for a cost that is less than the firm's manual handling, envelopes and postage. Productivity improves when firms eliminate redundant manual processes.

QL #25 ACTION: Acquire firm accounts payable credit card with maximum cash rebate and transition all possible payables to automatic or managed charges.

QL #26: External Secure File Transfer: Portal/Encryption

When dealing with digital files, the most effective way to transfer them is electronically over the Internet either with email or through a portal. Many firms have emailed clients copies of tax returns and financial statements over the years.

Unfortunately, this is not the most secure method as the firm does not have control of the various Internet Service Providers and the relay servers between the firm's email server and the client's email account.

> "39% primarily deliver tax returns in a digital format and 15% of firms delivered the majority of their organizers digitally."- CPAFMA 2015 S........

While using a password on the file provides some level of security, there have long been vendors providing password "removal" services for Adobe PDF, Microsoft Word and Microsoft Excel files. There are also secure email delivery services including Citrix ShareFile, LeapFile, and CPASafeSend, but these are standalone products that do not natively integrate with the firm's other practice applications. Some states have also disallowed the transmission of any documents with certain personally identifiable information unless that information was redacted, which can also be cost prohibitive.

To resolve this issue, the accounting profession is in the process of transitioning towards today's portal solutions which allow for secure movement of files both to and from clients. Portals are secure websites, most often accessed through the firm's own website where a secured connection allows data to be uploaded and downloaded by both the firm and the client. Each client would have a unique directory access to the portal so there is no risk of seeing another client's file, which was a problem with early FTP (file transfer protocol) sites that were incapable of this. Selecting a portal requires analysis of the level of security provided by each vendor. For example, firm personnel need the ability to access single location clients and clients with multiple entities. In this way, the portal application can restrict access only to the personnel who are authorized to view and update the documents.

QL #26: External Secure File Transfer: Portal/Encryption

The most effective portals integrate directly with a firm's document management, workflow and tax applications as this reduces the training required and makes it easier to move files in and out of the portal. Firms should look at portal solutions that will notify the in-charge for a specific client whenever any new document is uploaded or downloaded to the portal, as well as maintain an audit trail of activity. If the firm does not have a document management application, some of the leading providers of the "canned" accounting firm websites provide a portal as part of their service. A comprehensive listing of accounting-specific website providers can be found at www.websites4accountants.com.

QL #26 ACTION: Acquire portal solution for all client file transfer and educate personnel and clients on usage.

QL #27: Standardized QB/Accounting Support

In the United States, QuickBooks is the most dominant small business accounting product on the market and will be the application that the majority of the firm's clients use. Therefore, it is obvious that the firm must become proficient with supporting QuickBooks. Unfortunately, one of the biggest wastes of time is when firms support too many older versions of the software, which often leads to incompatibilities that can corrupt the database and make it unusable for clients. Fixing these errors creates lost time that is seldom charged to clients and instead impacts the profitability on these jobs. Firms have found that it is significantly more productive to support no more than the two most recent versions and to either require the client to update their software or include the cost within the monthly service fee. Updating software versions should be a standard procedure as part of the firm's bookkeeping.

One area of difficulty is the licensing of QuickBooks which can be expensive if the firm has a large number of users. Many firms have figured out that a better and more cost effective method is to have personnel certified as QuickBooks ProAdvisors. Certification provides five discounted licenses through each certified ProAdvisor. Getting multiple personnel certified is easy today as it can all be done online.

While there has been a strong trend towards Cloud computing, QuickBooks online accounting product has traditionally not fared well. While there have been significant improvements in the past two years, QuickBooks Online sometimes lacks important capabilities that clients rely upon. This has led to hosting companies such as RightNetworks delivering full versions of QuickBooks Professional on the Internet, and allowing providers such as Intacct and Xero to make inroads into the accounting market. We believe that QuickBooks online will narrow the features gap within the next two years. We suggest firms monitor these providers closely as web-based accounting allows both the firm and the client to access their information on any mobile device, which is the direction we expect the industry to go in the long term.

QL #27 ACTION: Designate one QuickBooks ProAdvisor for every five licenses required and actively monitor web-based accounting products

---

QL #28: Centralized Contact Administration

Many firms today maintain contact information within multiple applications such as practice management, Outlook, tax systems, and other marketing and CRM (customer relationship management) programs. Too often, a significant amount of time is wasted in firms pulling contact information together, reconciling and verifying lists for mailings, invitations, and even organizers. It is critical that firms centralize the updating of contact information for consistency.

> *"91% of firms have a centralized contact management list; 67% of firms maintained this list in their practice management application."* - CPAFMA 2015 Survey

For example, tax personnel, who are often the first to be made aware of a change, may make the change within their tax program and not pass the change to others. All changes, from every source, need to be sent to administration where one person can update ALL databases for consistency. Many firms utilize a client contact form on their intranet that can be routed to the administrative department via email. This person is then trained to update all applications.

In the next few years, the number of different databases a firm maintains will reduce as the major vendors integrate their products around a central contact list, which will be your practice management application. The latest products from CCH and Thomson Reuters function on SQL databases and can be integrated with Microsoft Exchange such that any changes made in practice can be also made in Outlook. If the firm is also using the same tax vendor as

> *"Email has become the primary means of communicating with clients in 87% of firms"* - AAA 2013 Survey

their practice management vendor, the new versions also can be integrated so that firms can access one contact list. Some firms will utilize a dedicated CRM application but we recommend this just be utilized by the marketing department and for individual marketing campaigns.

QL #28: Centralized Contact Administration

We anticipate the core users in the firm will rely on the contact data within time and billing that is linked to their other applications. Procedures need to be in place to avoid inconsistencies with best practices pointing to a central person updating all necessary databases.

QL #28A ACTION: Create a standard contact form incorporating all current contact database information and implement a centralized process to update all databases concurrently, particularly the practice management system used by the firm.

QL #28B ACTION: If using an older Time and Billing system, evaluate new practice management applications with superior integration. Plan to upgrade soon.

QL #29: Mandated Training Program/Accountability

For many firms, the ability to identify, standardize and implement best practices is the last remaining competitive advantage in business today as communications tools and access to technology have become available to everyone. To take advantage of the continuous stream of innovation and opportunities, firms must adopt a "learning culture." This requires a formal process to capture and standardize best practices in every department within the firm so that every person can take advantage of them.

All firms have personnel that are 10%, 20%, or even 50% more productive than other team members. These individuals have figured out how to optimize the firm's processes and the use of the applications to service clients more efficiently. Unfortunately, these people sometimes leave and that knowledge and experience leaves with them, so the solution is to have them document their best practices. In QL#20, we discussed a detailed process of how this can be done to develop the audit procedures manual. This process should be applied to every department within the firm so they can capture firm knowledge, which would be placed on the firm's intranet as the first major step towards knowledge management.

Firms must then have a formal training program to ensure that new hires meet the minimum production standards for core applications and a continuing training process to educate them on the specific applications and procedures they will need to be successful in their positions. They should also poll their personnel annually about what areas that training may be needed. Many firms develop a needs assessment form for their training curriculum as part of overall learning initiatives. Samples of such forms can be found at www.QuantumOfPaperless.com. In addition, there are articles dealing specifically with training for accounting firms in the article archive at that site.

QL #29: Mandated Training Program/Accountability

While larger firms (usually more than 75 personnel) have the resources to designate a person in the training coordinator role, smaller firms must allocate hours to specific personnel to manage the firm's training program. It is critical that these people be given chargeable credit for working on these projects otherwise they will be pushed down the priority list. By allocating specific hours and reviewing progress on a monthly basis, the firm can also make those personnel accountable for their training responsibilities.

> **QL #29 ACTION:** Have firm personnel complete a learning needs assessment form with the goal of developing a standard curriculum and a departmental curriculum. Designate hours and accountability for the firm's learning program and end-user support.

QL #30: Independent Security Review/Monitoring/Training

Going "paperless" means that all firm files and client data will be digitally stored on the firm's network, which is almost always accessible to firm personnel via internal workstations and remotely via the Internet. The firm has a fiduciary responsibility to protect this data from anyone not specifically authorized to view it. Proper security is VERY difficult for any internal network administrator to guarantee as few have the experience and ongoing training to implement security settings optimally the first time. Therefore, all "one shot" implementations of firewalls, WiFi Routers, virtual private networks, and other security settings should be outsourced to an organization that has experienced personnel dedicated to security. In many cases, these providers can also deliver ongoing monitoring and maintenance of the firm's firewall, Internet connectivity, and provide security guidance and personnel training. We recommend all firms conduct annual security training for all staff on today's most common cybersecurity threats.

The firm's security infrastructure can then be verified by an independent security consultant every few years, or whenever a major change in the firm's network infrastructure takes place. If there is not a security consultant locally, three vendors with accounting firm experience in North America are Arxis Technology (ArxisTechnology.com), McMillen Group (McMillenGroup.com) and Xcentric (Xcentric.com).

QL #30 ACTION: Have an independent security consultant/network integrator review firewall, anti-virus, spam, and physical security at least every three years or whenever a major change is made to the firm's infrastructure and mandate annual cybersecurity training for all firm personnel.

QL #31: Develop Monthly IT "Flash" Reports

Most firms have a line partner or firm administrator overseeing the firm's information technology department. These people may have an interest in information technology, but their primary responsibility lies in other production areas. They need a way to efficiently oversee the firm's IT initiatives.

That tool is a monthly IT flash report which is a one-page summary that monitors progress on the firm's core IT performance indicators. This form, usually done on a spreadsheet, should monitor items such as disk usage and processor performance on each server, Internet bandwidth, verify that antivirus and other updates are done properly, the status of helpdesk support calls, and list the core initiatives assigned to the IT department to monitor progress. While the IT person will initially have to explain the status of each item and what it means, after a few months, the director/administrator will be able to review it similar to the way a financial statement is reviewed. A sample form and article describing this in more detail can be found at www.QuantumOfPaperless.com.

QL #31 ACTION: Have internal/external IT personnel provide a monthly IT Flash Report that monitors the current technology infrastructure and status of ongoing projects.

QL #32: Updated Strategic Plan/Budget

We have all heard the saying that if you don't know where you are going, you'll end up going nowhere (or... you won't ever get there). Unfortunately, many accounting firms do not do a good job of integrating their information technology requirements into the firm's overall strategic vision. Information technology impacts virtually every aspect of accounting firm production and is usually the biggest expense after your personnel costs. Accordingly, it should be managed as the critically important asset that it is. This is one case where firms need to do exactly what they advise their clients to do and that is to manage information technology with a detailed budget that ties into the firm's strategic plan.

Reviewing the Quantum Leaps in this guide will help you formalize the IT components of your strategic plan so that you can then develop your IT budget. The most effective budgets actually begin by analyzing *last* year's numbers and breaking them down by applications, services, equipment and any other licenses required and then projecting all recurring items three years into the future. This establishes an IT "baseline" that the other owners and managers can understand is required just to keep the doors open. By running out the budget at least three years, the firm can project when new servers and desktop computers (which have a projected four to five-year life) will need to be replaced, as well as plan for laptops that must be replaced every three years. This format also allows for new initiatives and "one shot" items to be broken out and managed separately by individual line items which is much easier for owners to evaluate the ROI (return on investment). As specific servers reach the end of their functional life, it is imperative that firms also evaluate the cost of moving those applications individually to the cloud, which the budget is helpful for monitoring. For firms where their entire server infrastructure is nearing the end of life, hosted cloud providers should also be considered as they include IT staffing, support, updates, backup and disaster recovery into a fixed monthly fee per user, allowing the firm to focus on the practice of accounting instead of worrying about IT.

QL #32: Updated Strategic Plan/Budget

Having a detailed budget will allow the firm to calculate the average cost per workstation, which can then be added into the calculation whenever a new person is hired. Industry statistics point to firms spending between $6,500 and $8,500 per seat each year when all costs are taken into account or 5% for single office firms, 6% for multi-office firms that average approximately $135,000 net production per person.

> **QL #32 ACTION:** Download/populate budget template for previous year and project for next three years. Identify and focus on one core initiative in each department through completion.

Next Steps

To optimize the value of this guide, we recommend you review and set a preliminary prioritization to every item on the following Quantum Leap Quick List while you are reading the guide. You will come back to this list at later times to identify and target those projects the firm should be working on. An Excel version of this document can be downloaded from www.QuantumOfPaperless.com.

Once you have read this entire guide we suggest you review your prioritization with your entire team that should have completed their own copy of this form based on their individual perceptions, which will help the firm develop a firm wide listing which can then be prioritized. By selecting one or two projects in each department and focusing on those items through completion, the firm will make progress as opposed to trying to do too many things at once and not getting anywhere.

	Quantum Leap Quick List	Priority	Notes:
QL #1	Identify all tax professionals and document the number of oversize monitors that will be needed to bring all users up to the screen capacity of at least three monitors.		
QL #2	Purchase dedicated production scanners attached to workstations for administrative department to promote centralized scanning and train professional staff on utilizing workgroup and individual scanners for capturing physical paper documents.		

	Quantum Leap Quick List	Priority	Notes:
QL #3	Maintain laptop and desktop inventory to identify annual replacement requirements and purchase name brand business-class workstations in as large a lot as possible to promote standardization.		
QL #4	Inventory file servers and identify projected replacement cycle considering opportunities to utilize web-based solutions or consolidate servers if experienced integrators are available. Outsource all "one shot" projects to integrators with depth of personnel and experience with multiple implementations after evaluating which applications are more appropriate in a hosted/cloud environment.		
QL #5	Have your personnel verify that ALL data is being backed up, verified and stored offsite on at least a daily basis and that at least one person from *each* department is knowledgeable on how to find and restore a file. Ensure that all media that is moved physically offsite is encrypted to be in compliance with your State's cyber security laws.		

	Quantum Leap Quick List	Priority	Notes:
QL #6	Standardize purchases of new computers on Windows 10 for firm stability and verify all workstations have adequate RAM to handle multiple monitors and applications.		
QL #7	Verify the firm's audit/accounting applications are supported on the current Microsoft Office version and plan transition and training to one common version as part of firmwide roll out.		
QL #8	Standardize procedures to verify that all workstation and server security updates are automated and completed on a timely basis.		
QL #9	Identify the number of personnel that will work out of the office one day per week or more. Determine the expected number of concurrent users within the next two years so that you can implement the appropriate solution today including use of tablets and smartphones for remote access.		
QL #10	Implement dual Internet connections with different providers and re-negotiate your contract for bandwidth and pricing every 18-24 months.		

	Quantum Leap Quick List	Priority	Notes:
QL #11	Evaluate the best vendor in your region of operations and use a digital cellular connection either through an external MiFi device or smartphone "hotspot."		
QL #12A	Capture faxes and voicemail digitally at the root source and make available securely in Outlook via the Internet.		
QL #12B	Implement collaboration tools and train personnel on use.		
QL #13	Setup firm intranet to host firm knowledge and resources that are not part of a production application or document management system and add dashboard products to monitor KPIs.		
QL #14	Transition firm files to a document management application.		
QL #15A	Update firm document retention policy to include electronic documents and annually remind all personnel on firm retention policies.		
QL #15B	Evaluate firm's document retention cycle and promote accountability for cleaning out obsolete files.		
QL #16	Implement a digital workflow system to track due dates, status of returns, staffing on projects and links to source documents.		

	Quantum Leap Quick List	Priority	Notes:
QL #17	Purchase adequate production scanner and implement scanning applications to organize and optimize the importing of tax information.		
QL #18	Formalize process to have clients transfer files electronically.		
QL #19	Develop detailed departmental procedure manuals, update annually and provide ongoing training.		
QL #20	Outfit audit teams with appropriate digital tools and training to work effectively in the field.		
QL #21	Hire formal digital audit efficiency organization and document processes within audit procedures manual.		
QL #22	Mandate daily time entry, release and posting and provide training on daily billing processes.		
QL #23	Standardize all firm financial reporting to digital format and electronic delivery/notification to all recipients.		
QL #24	Setup online banking for daily account review and implement check scanning technology for daily remote deposit.		

	Quantum Leap Quick List	Priority	Notes:
QL #25	Acquire firm accounts payable credit card with maximum cash rebate and transition all possible payables to automatic or managed charges.		
QL #26	Acquire portal solution for all client file transfer and educate personnel and clients on usage.		
QL #27	Designate one QuickBooks ProAdvisor for every five licenses required and actively monitor web-based accounting products.		
QL #28A	Create a standard contact form incorporating all current contact database information and implement a centralized process to update all databases concurrently, particularly the practice management system used by the firm.		
QL #28B	If using an older Time and Billing system, evaluate new practice management applications with superior integration. Plan to upgrade soon.		

	Quantum Leap Quick List	Priority	Notes:
QL #29	Have firm personnel complete a learning needs assessment form with the goal of developing a standard curriculum and a departmental curriculum. Designate hours and accountability for the firm's learning program and end-user support.		
QL #30	Have an independent security consultant/network integrator review firewall, anti-virus, spam, and physical security at least every three years or whenever a major change is made to the firm's infrastructure and mandate annual cybersecurity training for all firm personnel.		
QL #31	Have internal/external IT personnel provide a monthly IT Flash Report that monitors the current technology infrastructure and status of ongoing projects.		
QL #32	Download/populate budget template for previous year and project for next three years. Identify and focus on one core initiative in each department through completion.		

2016 CPAFMA Information Technology Survey Findings

The CPA Firm Management Association (CPAFMA.org) targets the improvement of the internal operations of today's medium and larger sized CPA firms, with over 1,000 North American members. They conducted their first comprehensive technology survey with the goal of identifying the applications, products and processes utilized in this market. Where possible, the survey attempted to identify which applications firms are moving to in the cloud compared to traditionally on-premise managed solutions. The survey was conducted in January 2016, with 140 members participating, 90% of which had between 11 and 149 personnel and almost half being multi-office. The findings of the survey are summarized below and were presented via webcast on February 26, 2016 which was recorded and available to member firms.

As an Advisory Board Member and Firm Administrator member for over 28 years I would strongly encourage you to join if you are not already a member. The value and benefits I have received in regards to networking and CPAFMA resources have been immeasurable and directly impacted my personal consulting expertise.

2016 CPAFMA IT Survey Findings

Server Infrastructure: 77% of respondent firms still manage their own servers, and while 71% have servers located in their own firm office, 6% have chosen to move them to a colocation facility which offers more robust security, power and Internet bandwidth (with providers including ViaWest, IO, Barracuda). 18% of the firms transitioned to hosted cloud providers (15 to Xcentric, three to IV Desk and one each to Nuvodia, Cloud9, VNet, Cetrom, and Welcome Networks. The survey found 5% of participant firms using their accounting vendor cloud solutions with five on Thomson Reuters Virtual Office and two on CCH's Axcess cloud.

Server Virtualization: Virtualization was a very strong trend with 72% of the firms adopting this technology which simply stated, runs each application in its own "virtual server" providing great stability for accounting applications by minimizing conflicts. VMware was the preferred choice of 45% of respondents, followed by 17% of firms choosing Citrix Xen, and 10% selecting Microsoft Hyper V. Interestingly, with all the hype surrounding VDI (Virtual Desktops), none of the CPAFMA respondents had implemented this solution.

Network Utilities: The technology survey also identified various systems and maintenance applications utilized by peers:

- **Antivirus/Malware**: 17 firms (15% of respondents) stated they had been impacted by a virus, malware or ransomware that caused significant downtime in the past twelve months. The two top antivirus solutions utilized in firms were MacAfee (32 firms) and Symantec (29), followed by ESET (8), AVG (7), TrendMicro (7), Vipre (4) and Barracuda (3) with roughly one-third of respondents opting for the cloud-based products which are trending.
- **Backup Options:** While 12% of respondents still utilized tape backups, 48% backed up to hard disks, which we have seen to be more reliable and easier to restore files when needed. Half of member firms backed data up offsite via Internet-based solutions.
- **Data Backup/Archival Solutions:** Member firms are using a wide variety of data backup applications with no one product garnering any significant lead. This is evidenced by the top ten products; Datto (8 firms), VMware Veeam (7), Dell AppAssure (6), Acronis (5), Symantec/Veritas BackupExec (4), Mozy (3), EVault(2), Carbonite (2), Arcserve (2), and ShadowProtect (2).

Workstations: Dell still leads the pack for desktop brands with 62% of respondents making them the first choice followed 23% by HP and 9% by Lenovo. Studies done in the past pointed to a 26% reduction in the total cost of workstation ownership when firms standardized on one primary model. For laptop brands, Dell (58%), HP (20%), and Lenovo (17%) continued to be the major brands. The most popular laptop configuration was a 15" with full keyboard including a full ten key pad at 59% of respondents followed by 25% of firms buying 17" models as their standard, compared to only 11% selecting the smaller and lighter 14"-15" laptops without an integrated ten key.

Workstation Software: It comes as no surprise that Microsoft Windows is the dominant operating system (with no responding firms standardizing on Apple iOS). Windows 7 was the standard in 86 firms (75%) followed by 16 firms using Windows 8.x and 12 listing Windows 10. The survey also found that more than one third of the respondents already had or were planning on transitioning to Windows 10 in 2016. 68% of CPAFMA respondents utilized Internet Explorer as their browser followed by 26% utilizing Google Chrome and 3% using Mozilla FireFox. Microsoft Office 2010 was the dominant version of Office with 59 respondents (51%) followed by 45 firms on Office 2013 (39%) and seven firms on Office 2007 (6%). Four firms had transitioned to Office 2016, which we anticipate will begin the transition of Microsoft software to more annual subscription based pricing. Adobe continues to be the dominant PDF program with 59 firms (53%) standardizing on Adobe 11 followed by 31 firms (27%) using Adobe 10. Seventeen firms (15%) had transitioned to Adobe 12/DC, which we expect the five firms that were still utilizing Adobe 9 will have to transition to this year.

Monitors: The survey specifically asked for the standard tax desktop setup which pointed to 54% (61 firms) utilizing Triple monitors as the standard. This was followed by 22% (25 firms) using Dual Oversize monitors greater than 20" and 19% (22 firms) using Dual Standard monitors less than 20".

Tablets: 34% of peer firm provided tablets to all partners and 10% provided them to all managers, but only 3% provided them to all staff. The survey found that two out of three tablets purchased were Apple iPads with the remaining third being Android (Dell, Samsung, Motorola) and Windows (Microsoft Surface) variations.

Smartphones: 60% of peer firms provided all partners and 24% provided managers with Smartphones, with the majority (79%) being Apple iPhones and the remainder being Android (Primarily Samsung Galaxy) smartphones. 44% of firms provided a stipend which varied greatly between firms.

Scanner Technology: Fujitsu was the vendor of choice for 57% of respondents for their production scanners followed by 28% of peers selecting Canon. The survey found that 75% of respondents (84 firms) had implemented centralized scanning and 74 of these firms estimated they scanned 70% or more of all documents in administration. 69 member firms had also implemented distributed/shared scanners and 62 had rolled out some individual scanners, but less than half of these firms (27 firms) estimated that 50% or more of the scanning was done on these units.

CPA Practice Applications: Below we summarize the administrative applications which CPAFMA peer firms utilize to run their internal operations. The number of firms selecting either on-premise or cloud applications have been identified where possible.

- **Practice Management:** 86 firms (52% of respondents) utilized CCH's Practice Management of which 14 were in the cloud either privately or through their Axcess Suite. Thomson Reuters had 43 peer firms using their Practice CS application, of which 15 firms were in the cloud or hosted in Thomson's Virtual Office. OfficeTools also made a good showing as it was selected by 23 firms, evenly dispersed across the spectrum of firm sizes.
- **Payroll**: For producing firm payroll, 35 firms utilized Paychex, followed by ADP (23 firms) and Intuit (12 Online and 4 QuickBooks internal). Seven firms utilized Thomson's Accounting CS and two utilized their MyPay solutions.
- **CPE**: Practice Management applications are also the tool of choice for CPE Tracking with 42 firms utilizing CCH and 33 utilizing Thomson Reuters' tools (of which 23 utilized Thomson Learning/Virtual Office and 10 used their on-premise Practice CS. Not surprising was that a significant number of firms (25) continued to utilize Excel spreadsheets for tracking CPE.
- **HR**: HR Management is another area where there was a wide variety of applications with no one product being dominant. ADP's HRIS was used by nine firms, followed by Bamboo with six firms, and then Halogen, Paychex, and Paylocity each had three firms. Fifteen other products were utilized by peer firms.
- **Intranet**: Microsoft SharePoint was the most dominant tool used by firms (27 firms) for intranet development followed by WordPress (five firms). Our consulting with CPAs has found that many firms still utilize an administrative drive or their document management application which was not reflected in the survey question.

- **CRM Tools**: Practice Management was the most dominant tool utilized for Customer Relationship Management with 58 firms using CCH and nine using Thomson Reuters, followed by 15 other distinct applications.
- **Website Maintenance**: While a large number of respondents maintained their own websites with local providers, CCH Sitebuilder led the survey respondents with 12 firms, followed by CPA Site Solutions (four firms) and WordPress and Thomson Web Builder CS utilized by two firms each.
- **Internal Accounting**: On Premise QuickBooks continues to be the dominant accounting product utilized by firms with 66 firms, followed by Sage/MAS with nine firms and Thomson CS with seven firms. The number of firms utilizing cloud providers for running their internal accounting was centered around QuickBooks Online/RightNetworks at 16 firms and Intacct with five.
- **Accounts Payable Management**: QuickBooks was also the primary tool used for managing payables with 59 on premise users and 14 in the cloud, followed by cloud-based Bill.com with 11 respondents. The second and third most prevalent products were Sage/MAS with nine firms and Thomson Reuters CS with four firms.
- **Expense Reports:** 15 firms utilized their Practice Management application for inputting expense reports which is a recommended practice with time entry. Surprisingly, only nine firms stated they utilized cloud based expense products [Tallie (4 firms), Expensify (2), Concur (2) and Bill.com (1)].
- **Scheduling:** Excel continues to be the dominant tool utilized for scheduling staff with 23 firms reporting they do so. This was followed by firms using Practice Management scheduling components [CCH (22) and Thomson (4)] or Outlook (four firms primarily between 11 and 24 members). ProStaff was utilized by 16 member firms which placed it at the top of the dedicated internal products and XCM Schedule was the most utilized cloud application with 11 firms using it.

Email/Groupware: Microsoft continues to be the dominant Groupware product utilized by 79 firms internally and by 37 firms that have transitioned to cloud based versions. In our consulting, this is one of the primary applications that firms transition to the cloud when they consider the cost of building and maintaining their own servers. Interestingly, four peer firms have moved their groupware to Google's platform. The survey also asked about the standard mailbox size that was allocated to users and found it fairly equally distributed: 23 Firms allowed 1Gb or less, 25 firms allowed between 1Gb and 5Gb, 16 firms allocated 5Gb, and 42 firms allocated more than 5Gb, which we see being due to Microsoft's hosted Exchange providing 50Gb to start.

Collaboration/Instant Messaging: Microsoft's Skype for Business (formerly Lync and Office Communicator) was the dominant application in this space with 28 member firms using it (15-cloud, 13-on-premise). There were also thirteen firms using IM through their phones with the most prevalent being ShoreTel (5 firms) and Mitel MiCollab (3 firms). Three of the four Google groupware users from the previous question also utilized Google Plus for their Instant Messaging.

Video Calling: 55 peer firms were using video calling with Microsoft Skype for Business/Lync again being the dominant product (22-cloud, 21 on-premise responses). Firms with dedicated video conferencing products listed LifeSize (4 firms), Zoom (2), Mitel (2), Vidyo (2) and five firms utilized GoToMeetings video calling capability.

Document Management: DM products were utilized by 97 firms with on-premise tools being more prevalent. CCH Document led the charts with 25 firms followed by five firms using Thomson File Cabinet and a variety of other local products: iChannel (3 firms), CCH Engagement (3), CaseWare (2), Lacerte DMS (2), eFileCabinet (2), and Laserfiche (2). For Cloud based products, Thomson's GoFileRoom led with 20 firms, followed by Acct1st utilized by three CPAFMA peers.

Portal/Secure Delivery Solutions: The top three portal solutions listed by respondents were CCH (39), Thomson (17) and iChannel (3), which we honestly expected to be higher if not for the number of firms using secured email tools. ShareFile garnered the top spot for delivery of secure email with 47 firms using it followed by LeapFile (5 firms) and CPA Safe Send (3 firms).

Tax Applications: This survey was combined with the previous SaaS/Cloud survey with the specific intent of identifying which applications are moving to the cloud as there have long been tax, document management portal and research tools available. Below we summarize the tax applications utilized with CPAFMA peer firms.

- **Individual/1040 Production**: CCH was the dominant tool used by respondents with 81 firms selecting it (including 20 in the cloud). This was followed by 24 firms Thomson's UltraTax (of which 8 were in the cloud) and their cloud-based GoTax RS (3 firms). Nine member firms utilized Lacerte with one being cloud-hosted, which it could not be determined if this was a private cloud or Intuit's Tax Online, which utilizes the Lacerte tax engine.

- **Business/Other Returns**: Not surprisingly CCH was dominant in this space with 82 firms (21 Cloud/Axcess) followed by Thomson Reuters UltraTax with 24 firms (of which seven were in the cloud). Six member firms selected Lacerte and three utilized Thomson's GoTax RS in the cloud.

- **Tax Bookmarking**: With the preponderance of firms selecting CCH for tax production it was no surprise the CCH FxScan was the most dominant bookmarking tool (55 firms), followed by Thomson Reuters' Source Document Scanning being utilized in eight peers. Three other tools utilized were SurePrep (6 firms), Tic Tie & Calculate (3), and Gruntworx (2).

- **Tax Scanning to OCR**: The majority of firms utilizing bookmarking were also using automatic input into the tax return, which was led by 46 CCH firms using AutoFlow. This was followed by seven firms that outsourced to SurePrep, and five to Thomson's GFR/SDS Products.

- **Dedicated Workflow**: While many firms traditionally utilized Practice Management Projects to track tax workflow, there has been a trend towards dedicated tools. The top three products that peer firms have transitioned to were XCM (23 firms), Thomson FirmFlow (22) and CCH Workstream (9), which is an area we see a strong trend towards firms adopting in the next few years.

- **Tax Research/Forms**: Thomson's RIA Checkpoint was the dominant Research tool utilized by 79 peer firms, followed by 49 firms using CCH Intelliconnect, and 32 using BNA. With only 109 firms responding to this question, the numbers point to many firms having duplicate products, which should be evaluated to eliminate redundancy. For accessing tax forms, 55 respondents utilized CCH while 35 utilized RIA, and 24 had BNA's SuperForm product.

Audit and Accounting Applications: The. The survey also targeted assurance services to identify adoption of the following applications and utilities:

- **Audit Binder:** The dominant engagement binder application utilized by firms was CCH Engagement with 74 firms. Within these CCH respondents 14 firms stated they hosted their binder in the cloud, which would point to firms hosting their networks with Citrix or Windows Terminal Server as this is not anticipated to be part of the CCH Axcess suite for another two years. Sixteen firms utilized Caseware (with five also cloud hosted) and Thomson's Engagement was utilized by 13 member firms, with one utilizing their new cloud-based AdvanceFlow application which is part of Thomson's web-based audit suite.
- **Data Extraction:** While being touted by digital audit pundits for the past decade, only 20 firms utilized IDEA for data extraction (with only two utilizing the competitive ACL product). The vast majority of peer firms (50 responses) listed Excel as their data extraction tool and fifteen firms had transitioned to the ActiveData Excel add-on which appears to be the rising star.
- **Client Payroll:** While 20 firms outsourced payroll to ADP, 17 to QuickBooks Online, and four to Paychex, the majority still produced internal payroll primarily with QuickBooks (40 firms) and Thomson's CS/MyPay products (22 firms).
- **Depreciation:** CCH Fixed Assets was selected by 53 firms followed by 36 utilizing Thomson's Fixed Asset CS. Interestingly, eight CCH firms stated their depreciation was cloud-based, which would point to them being hosted by a third party, whereas Thomson had eleven firms using cloud based depreciation, which could be either hosted by a third party or their own Virtual Office. The other three products mentioned by peers were BNA FAS (10 firms) and AssetKeeper (7).
- **Remote Access Tools:** Microsoft Windows Terminal Server/RDS was utilized by 51 firms (47% of respondents) followed by 42 firms (40%) utilizing Citrix for remote access. The remainder of firms either did not have a remote access tool or utilized VPN, GoToMyPC, or LogMeIn. The survey found that only four firms had more than 80% of their employees

telecommute one day per week or more. Eleven firms estimated between a quarter and half of their staff worked remotely at least one day per week, and 25 firms stated that between 5%-25% telecommuted weekly, pointing to this being a distinct recruiting advantage to those firms that allow it.

IT Governance: The vast majority of peer firms (95 firms representing 83% of respondents) utilized a technology budget that was reviewed at least annually. Surprisingly, only 54% (61 firms) had a designated IT Committee. Of those that did have an IT Committee, 39% met monthly, 31% met quarterly, 22% annually/as needed and 8% met at least every other week.

IT Training Resources: The final technology survey question had respondents list the best training resources with the most firms selecting the accounting vendor user conferences: CCH (31 firms), Thomson Reuters (10), Xcentric (6), Sleeter (3), XCM (2). This was followed by 16 firms listing the CPAFMA National Symposium and/or Technology Fly-in and the AICPA TECH/Practitioners Symposium.

CPA Firm Management Association, formerly the Association for Accounting Administration (CPAFMA.org)

The mission and vision of the CPA Firm Management Association is to be a recognized leader in CPA firm practice management delivering valuable education and collaboration opportunities for those interested in elevating their practice and strategically growing their firms. CPAFMA will be a strategic enabler of relationships and provider of valuable connections, resources and education to support holistic CPA firm practice management in areas such as strategy/partner issues, human resources, technology, finance, marketing and business development, in-firm communications, client service, operations and facilities.

CPAFMA 2015 Benchmarking

Paperless Office Best Practices Survey

The Association for Accounting Administration (CPAAdmin.org) conducted their 2015 paperless benchmarking survey to find out the status of paperless office practices in accounting firms for the 2015 busy season. The survey has been conducted every two years beginning in 2003 to help identify trends in adopting "less paper" processes and 102 participated in this survey. It is recommended that firms have each member of the IT/management team complete the survey to help identify technology opportunities and assist the firm in prioritizing Quantum Leaps. A printable version of this survey can be found at www.QuantumOfPaperless.com

2015 CPAFMA Paperless Benchmark Survey	2013	2015
1. NEW: Tax: Does your firm utilize a digital workflow tool to manage tax return progress? -25% XCM Solutions -15% Thomson Reuters FirmFlow - 5% CCH Workstream - 3% Office Tools Professional - 3% Utilized their firm's Practice Management - 6% "Other" included Outlook, Doc-It, Conarc, and custom applications	NEW	59%
2. Tax: Is your firm delivering the MAJORITY of your Organizers via digital means? - 9%: Thomson Reuters Portal CS/GFR Portal - 4%: "Other" - 2% CCH Portal	14%	15%
3. Tax - Does your firm PRIMARILY scan client source documents (W2, 1099, etc.) at the front end of the process when the return is received and/or prior to review (mid-level scanning) so they are utilized onscreen?	78%	75%

2015 CPAFMA Paperless Benchmark Survey	2013	2015
4. Tax - Is your firm utilizing internal software or external services to **organize/bookmark** scanned client source documents into a standard PDF Format? -41% CCH FxScan -13% SurePrep - 8% GFR/TR Source Document Scanning - 9% "Other" (Doc-IT, , Adobe)	57%	**70%**
5. Tax - Is your firm using software that utilizes Optical Character Recognition to automatically transfer data from scanned source documents into your tax program? -27% CCH AutoFlow -10% SurePrep - 6% Thomson Reuters Source Document Scanning - 4% Other *2013 Question asked only for "Internal" software for OCR	33%	**47%**
6. Tax - Does your firm primarily deliver tax returns in a digital format? -11% CCH Portal - 9% Thomson Reuters - 6% ShareFile - 6% Physical CDs/Flashdrives - 7% "Other" Portals/DM Systems	35%	**39%**
7. Tax: What is the primary monitor configuration for tax professionals on their desktop? -55% Triple Monitors -24% Dual-Oversize (at least one screen 20" or greater) -20% Dual-Standard (both screens 19" or less) - 1% Quadruple	63% use more than traditional dual	80% use more than traditional dual
8. NEW: TAX - Do the majority of your tax personnel utilize at least one monitor in a vertical, "portrait" mode?	NEW	**45%**
9. NEW: Tax - Do you plan to use a digital eSignature tool for tax returns this busy season? (Note: wide variety of products listed with Right Signature listed most often-5 firms)	NEW	**31%**
10. Audit - Does your firm primarily link its audit applications to its tax application to digitally transfer trial balance information?	68%	**68%**

2015 CPAFMA Paperless Benchmark Survey	2013	2015
11. Audit - Do your personnel working outside the office access firm applications and information via a remote connection (SaaS, Virtual Private Network, Citrix/WTS) more than 50% of the time?	70%	77%
12. Audit - Do your auditors carry multiple monitors in the field?	63%	74%
13. Audit-Do auditors carry any of the following into the field the majority of the time? - 57% Scanners (32% in 2013) - 22% Printers (15% in 2013) - 9% Multi-Function Devices (10% in 2013) *Some firms responded to two or three devices	63%	67%
14. Audit: Does your Firm utilize a single vendor for audit programs/engagement binders? - 21% CCH Engagement with CCH Knowledge Coach - 13% TR Engagement CS/Advance Flow with PPC Smart Practice	NEW	34%
15. Audit: Do your auditors utilize data extraction tools on the majority of their engagements? (Check All that Apply): -45% Excel -21% IDEA - 7% Information Active/ActiveData	58%	74%
16. Audit: Do your auditors utilize a digital audit scheduling tool? - 19% utilizes ProStaff or Staff Track "dedicated" scheduling tool which was down from 29% in 2013 *Please note that 31% utilized Excel in 2015, down from 39% in 2013, and 14% utilized Practice Management, which was not tracked in 2013.*	*29%	19%
17. Accounting: Does your firm utilize web-based accounting products for client service?	71%	52%
18. Administration - Does your firm utilize an intranet to store firm wide information (i.e. personnel manual and internal firm procedures)? -28% utilized Microsoft SharePoint -21% utilized Document Management -23% "Other: Yammer, Engagement, HR, Custom	64%	72%
19. Administration - Does your firm deliver firm *internal* financial and management reports electronically?	75%	84%

2015 CPAFMA Paperless Benchmark Survey	2013	2015
20. Administration - Does your firm have an electronic document destruction procedure to ensure deletion of outdated electronic files on the network?	53%	**71%**
21. Administration - Does your firm use a firm-wide document management program for archival of all final tax returns, financial reports, and firm correspondence? -31% CCH Document (22% on Premise, 9% Axcess) -12% Thomson GoFileRoom -11% Thomson File Cabinet CS - 6% Conarc iChannel - 6% Engagement Binders (CCH/Caseware) - 3% Doc-It and 3% eFileCabinet	66%	**78%**
22. Administration - Does your firm *pay the majority of* accounts payables via electronic means such as credit card, online bank draft, or online service (Bank ACH, Bill.com, etc.)?	50%	**52%**
23. Administration - Does you firm utilize a remote check scanner in your office to deposit client checks?	63%	**76%**
24. Administration - Does your firm deliver digital payroll stubs via secure email or portal?	58%	**70%**
25. Administration: Are expense reports submitted electronically?	33%	**47%**
26. Practice Management - Do owners/managers receive internal management reports electronically (via email or by looking them up on the computer)?	66%	**84%**
27. Practice Management - Do firm personnel utilize information dashboards within your Practice Management application to update internal reporting information?	48%	**33%**
28. Practice Management - Are the majority of invoices prepared onscreen rather than completed on *manual* billing sheets?	68%	**67%**
29. Practice Management - Does your firm deliver client invoices electronically?	44%	**35%**
30. NEW: Practice management –Does your firm accept digital payment for services (check all that apply)? -81% Credit Card (firm entered) -51% ACH (firm entered) -15%Credit Card via Website (client entered)	NEW	**88%**

2015 CPAFMA Paperless Benchmark Survey	2013	2015
31. NEW: Practice management –Does your firm have a centralized contact management list accessible by all personnel (Check all that apply)? -67% Practice management contacts (stored in time and billing) -32% Outlook -18% Other *2013 Question: Does your firm maintain a contact/prospect list in its practice management or groupware application?	*82%	**NEW** **91%**
32. Communications - Does your firm provide internet enabled devices (other than smart phones) for senior management working outside the office (i.e. tablets, netbooks, etc.)?	33%	**54%**
33. Communications - Has your firm implemented Unified Messaging Technology for all staff (voice message/integrated fax delivered electronically via email)?	66%	**62%**
34: NEW: Communications: Does your firm utilize a collaboration tool which includes instant messaging? -17% Lync -13% Skype -18% Other (Phone, Yammer, ShoreTel, Google, Cisco, Jabber) *2013 Question: Does your firm utilize instant messaging?	*27%	**47%**
35. Communications: Does your firm utilize video calling/conferencing?	37%	**54%**
36. Technology - Does your firm backup all firm data to the Internet (web-based storage/archival) on at least a monthly basis? -56% Daily/Work Days -7% Weekly -3% Monthly	57%	**67%**
37. Technology - Does your firm utilize a SharePoint server or Lotus Notes knowledge database?	31%	**42%**
38. Technology – Has your firm transitioned to a virtualized server environment? -51% VMware -13% Microsoft HyperV or "Did Not Know"	56%	**64%**

2015 CPAFMA Paperless Benchmark Survey	2013	2015
39. Has your firm implemented a Mobile Device Management application to secure your mobile devices and access to the firm's network? -7% AirWatch -7% Exchange/Active Sync -5% Maas360 -16% Other (Good, Meraki, Mobile Iron, Citrix or "Did Not Know" NOTE: 3% Provided Firm Issued Smart Phones (2nd Phone)	NEW	**35%**
40. Does your firm utilize remote access tools to connect to client computers to provide support, training or remote work? -16% LogMeIn - 9% Go to Meeting/GoToAssist -22% Other (Join.me, TeamViewer, RAS, Lync, etc.)	NEW	**47%**

QL BONUS ACTION: Have firm owners complete blank survey found at www.QuantumOfPaperless.com to document their perception and compare their results to CPAFMA Survey findings.

About the Author: **Roman H. Kepczyk, CPA.CITP, CGMA**

Roman H. Kepczyk, CPA.CITP, CGMA is Director of Consulting for Xcentric, LLC. His primary focus is helping firms throughout North America effectively use information technology by implementing digital best practices and directing them towards today's "less paper" or Digital CPA firm by optimizing their tax, audit, client services, and administrative production workflows.

He has spent the past twenty years consulting exclusively with CPA firms and prior to that, ten years with the CPA firm of Henry & Horne, (Arizona's largest regional firm) where he was the partner in charge of the firm's Management Advisory Services and Microcomputer Consulting practices. Roman also served as the firm's Administrative partner where he oversaw Internal Accounting, Marketing, Human Resources, and was responsible for the creation and implementation of the firm's technology plan and budget.

Roman was named by INSIDE Public Accounting as one of the profession's Most Recommended Consultants every year from 2004 through 2015 and Accounting Today's Most Influential People for the years 2015, 2014, 2013, 2011, and 2000 through 2005. CPA Practice Advisor also named him as one of the profession's Top 25 Thought Leaders every year of the list from 2011through 2016.

Roman is an AAAPM and an Advisory Board Member to the CPA Firm Management Association (CPAFMA.org formerly AAA-Association for Accounting Administration) and has served on the Board of Directors of the Arizona Society of CPAs. He is a past member of the AICPA PCPS Executive Committee and past Chairman of the AICPA's Information Technology Executive Committee.

On a technical level, Roman is an AICPA Certified Information Technology Professional and a Lean Six Sigma certified Black Belt. He regularly writes columns for the CPA Practice Advisor, PPC's Audit and Accounting Update, the AAA Report/Insights, and various AICPA publications. He authored and maintains the technology chapters for the PPC MAP Handbook, PPC Guide to Paperless Engagements, and sections of the AICPA MAP Handbook, as well as co-authored the 2003 AICPA Top Technologies Guide when he was Chairman of the AICPA's Top Technologies initiative.

Accounting Firm Process Optimization (FPO) and Virtual CIO

> **Fast Track your Firm's Digital Workflow Adoption**
>
> **Xcentric's Virtual CIO and FPO Review Processes:**

Roman H. Kepczyk, CPA,CITP, CGMA, LSS BB partners directly with accounting firms as their *independent* outsourced IT resource to ensure your firm is aware of, and taking advantage of today's information technology best practices. This is done via the Virtual CIO and FPO/ExSTRM Review (Executive Strategic Technology Resource Management) processes which entails one-day onsite interviewing and educating key members of the firm's IT, Tax, Audit, Client Services, Marketing, and Administrative Departments, concluding with a detailed written document that outlines the firm's future technology path. The FPO/ExSTRM Review provides firm owners confidence they are making the right technology decisions and have the right resources to optimally serve their client base. The Virtual CIO process expands the FPO Review to a year-long program to proactively monitor progress towards the firm's strategic technology initiatives to ensure "less paper" adoption. To date, Roman has partnered with over 325 accounting entities including 30 of the Top 100 CPA Firms.

To learn more about how Xcentric Consulting can assist your firm:

Website   **www.xcentric.com/consulting**

Email   **Roman@xcentric.com**

          Roman H. Kepczyk, CPA.CITP, CGMA
Mail   **Xcentric, LLP**
          3015 Windward Plaza, Suite 500
          Alpharetta, GA 30005

Sign up for our **FREE** blog: **http://xcentric.com/blog**

Customized Learning Coming To a Location Near You

Roman H. Kepczyk, CPA.CITP, CGMA, LSS BB has presented lively and highly rated accounting information training to thousands of CPAs and can bring this education directly into your firm in a format customized specifically to your group's needs. Bring your team up to speed quickly on the latest information technologies from one of INSIDE Public Accounting's Most Recommended Consultants for the past eleven years running. Previous topics have included:

Accounting Firm Digital Best Practices

Workflow: CPA Firm Digital EcoSystem

Quantum of Gadgets

Cloud Computing in Your Future

Impacts of the AICPA Top Technologies

Strategic Technology Management for Accounting Firms

Intranets, Document, Portal and Knowledge Management

IT Governance: Security Training for Firm Personnel

Today's Security and Privacy Concerns

Optimizing Remote Working Technologies

Find out when we will be in your area and read about updated sessions:

http://xcentric.com/roman

Roman H. Kepczyk, CPA.CITP, CGMA, LSS BB
is **your** technology partner! 678-495-0508 (roman@xcentric.com)

<u>Notes</u>

_____

_____

_____

_____

_____

_____

_____

_____

_____

_____

_____

_____

_____

_____

_____

_____

_____

_____

Notes

_____

_____

_____

_____

_____

_____

_____

_____

_____

_____

_____

_____

_____

_____

_____

_____

Made in the USA
San Bernardino, CA
01 March 2016